CONSULTING SPIRIT
A Doctor's Experience with
Practical Mediumship

Dr. Ian D. Rubenstein

ANOMALIST BOOKS
San Antonio * New York

An Original Publication of ANOMALIST BOOKS

Consulting Spirit
Copyright © 2011 by Ian D. Rubenstein
ISBN: 1933665556

Cover image: Punam Rubenstein

Book design by Seale Studios

For information, go to anomalistbooks.com, or write to:
Anomalist Books, 5150 Broadway #108, San Antonio, TX
78209

For Frances, who now knows the truth.
Possibly.

Contents

Preface

Some very strange events started happening to me a few years ago and you may be interested in reading about them—just in case they start happening to you, too. One of the reasons why I've written this book is because, when I began to have these experiences, I would have welcomed reading something like this, detailing how someone else had coped. The other reason is "they" told me to. If you want to know who "they" are, you're going to have to read on. It's all true—well, I mean it all really happened. Whatever the ultimate truth behind it is, I'll leave for you to figure out—I'm still working on it.

My story starts in the summer of 2003. I didn't know it at the time, but I was like a man standing on the edge of a cliff. This is the story of how I took a leap of faith off that cliff.

1

Like a Man on the Edge of a Cliff

It's not every day your dead grandfather comes to visit you. But that's what was happening to me now. Or at least, that's what my last patient of the morning, Keith Bishop, was saying.

"I've always been able to see spirit," he said, by way of explanation.

Spirit? Surely, he meant spirits. I must have misheard.

"Always?" I asked, archly. "How come you've never mentioned this before?"

"I've been seeing spirit ever since I was a child. It's not the sort of thing you'd normally tell your doctor, but this is important."

It just goes to show, you never can tell what life will throw at you. Because, so far, it had seemed like any other day. I'd spent the morning seeing patients and I'd seen them all, apart from Keith, who'd had the last appointment of the morning and had turned up, eventually, 15 minutes late.

It's not unusual for patients to miss booked appointments without letting my staff know, so I have a rule: don't hang around for the last patient—they may never turn up.

Anyway, I had a few house calls to make, and I wanted to go for a swim during my lunch break. So I'd decided not to wait for Keith.

But as I'd tidied the papers on my desk, making ready to leave my office, I'd felt something like a short, sharp tap to the back of my head. And yet...it hadn't felt quite real. In fact the sensation had been just as if someone had pushed something quite forcefully into the back of my head—or rather into the back of my mind. With it had been a thought, a very powerful thought: "Just wait a few more moments."

So I'd sat there, wondering why I couldn't get a move on and wondering what to do next. Conscious that time was pressing, I'd started to get up off my chair...but felt as if I'd been pushed back down. Very peculiar.

Then Carol, one of the receptionists, had buzzed me on the phone.

"It's about Mr. Bishop. His secretary just rang to say he's on his way. He'll be here in a few minutes. Can you wait?"

"Yes," I'd said, feeling exasperated. "But I'm not waiting all day."

Keith Bishop had turned up within a couple of minutes: red-faced, panting, and full of apologies. He'd come to have his blood pressure checked, which meant I'd have wait a bit longer because he'd certainly need some time to cool down a little before I took it.

Keith had been my patient for the past 20 years or so. A bit of a schmoozer and a snazzy dresser, he ran a small PR agency and knew many people in the entertainment industry. His lifestyle was very high-pressured, as was his blood pressure, which was as bad as ever. I'd been telling him to calm down for years but we both knew he never would. He liked to drop a few famous names into our conversations and could be very entertaining.

In an effort to allow his blood pressure to settle, I'd asked him how things were going, what he'd been doing, and so on. And at first it had all seemed so normal.

But then our conversation had taken a decidedly weird turn when Keith, who'd been in full flow with the latest show biz gossip, had suddenly given me an odd look and said, "I hope you don't mind, Doctor, but I've got this man here and he says he knows you."

"What?" I'd said.

"Well, he says he's your grandfather—the one you never met. And he wants to tell you something."

Silence.

In 20 years of being a primary care physician, I thought I'd heard it all. To say I was taken aback would be putting it mildly. All sorts of things had crossed my mind, not least that Keith, always slightly neurotic, actually had more serious mental health problems than I'd realized. If this was a psychiatric case, then I was certainly not going to be able to go for my swim today.

I'd sat back in my chair, sighed inwardly and said, "Okay, Keith. What are you telling me?"

And that's how I came to be sitting in my office at the end of a busy clinic hearing about how he'd always been able to see spirit. And I was certain he'd said "spirit," not "spirits," which, for some reason, both puzzled and annoyed me in equal measure.

I thought, okay, get a grip and forget about the time. Let's see where this goes.

And I have to admit, I was intrigued. The grandfather I'd never met would be my mother's father and I'd been thinking about him rather a lot lately. I'd been having problems getting on with my parents and sister. This had caused a major family rift. The resulting row had drawn in my cousins, aunts, and uncles. My counseling training led me to believe that previous generations of my mother's family had sown the seeds of this current crisis. I reckoned my mother's parents, who had both died before I was born, had been key players.

"So, what does he want to say?" I asked.

Keith leaned forward. He was more animated than usual, his voice slightly breathless. He thrust his hands towards me in an open-palmed gesture, meaning trust me, this is important.

"This is how it works. I'll let him come through. He'll tell me what he wants to say and I'll pass it on to you. Just let my words flow and don't interrupt or ask any questions. If I say anything that might seem offensive, well, it's not me, it's him."

His gaze was direct, inquiring—was I open-minded enough to allow this to happen?

I nodded agreement. He had me hooked. All he had to do now was reel me in.

Keith appeared slightly distracted, as if trying to find the right words. Then he seemed to shift gear and proceeded to talk rapidly for about 20 minutes. He told me what had been happening in my family. He outlined my mother's behavior, its root causes, and reassured me things would eventually get better. He also told me my grandfather was very proud of my wider family's professional achievements and outlined these, too. He was completely accurate. But there was no way Keith could know all this.

Keith's demeanor changed and he became his usual self.

He looked at me quizzically.

"Was that all right, then? I hope I didn't say anything that upset you."

I reassured him that, although I was shocked, I'd found what he'd told me...well, interesting.

Keith looked relieved. "You know what? William, my spirit guide, is telling me *you* should be doing this."

I was puzzled. "Doing what?"

"Listening to spirit. William says you've always been aware of this, but you're like a man on the edge of a cliff. You need to step off the cliff and not worry about it. You won't fall, you know. Just let yourself go. They'll catch you."

Oh, really, I thought.

"Who's William?" I asked.

"William was my boss at the BBC. He was very good to me

when he was alive. Then he died and became my spirit guide."

The consultation had become surreal. At that point, having a spirit guide who used to be your old boss seemed a fairly reasonable proposition.

Keith got up to leave, pocketing his prescription. He paused at the door.

"By the way, did you know you have an older brother in spirit?"

Well, that was obviously ridiculous.

"You mean dead? No way. I have a sister who's four years younger than me. I've never had a brother."

Keith shook his head. "You do have a brother. Your mother had a miscarriage before you were born. He grew up in spirit."

He was right about the miscarriage, but I really didn't know what to make of this brother nonsense. After all, I knew many women who'd had early miscarriages. While I could just about buy into survival after death, the idea of fetuses that never made it growing up in some sort of spirit world just didn't make any sort of sense to me.

"He says he'll come and see you tonight at eleven o'clock."

With that, Keith left.

My receptionists had been worried about me. After all, they knew I don't usually hang around after clinic. And I'd spent almost an hour with Keith.

"Are you all right, Ian?" asked Carol, as I came into the receptionists' office.

I told her what had happened.

"Ooh," she said. "I love all that! Have you seen *Most Haunted* on TV?"

"No," I said. "I don't watch much TV."

I didn't know it at the time, but I'd just crossed over into my own personal Twilight Zone.

That evening after I got home, over dinner, I told Punam and the boys what had happened. We all laughed about it.

At half past ten, Punam yawned, stood up and said, "I'm going to bed."

She wrapped her dressing gown belt around her waist.

"When are you coming up?" she asked.

"I'll read for a bit in the attic. And wait for my brother to come and see me." I hoped I'd sounded dismissive.

Punam smiled. "Good luck, then." She gave me a kiss.

I lay on the settee in the attic looking up at my reflection in the window set into the sloping roof. Now, how did one prepare to greet a long-lost spirit brother? I closed my eyes and tried to calm my mind using a self-hypnosis technique I knew. At eleven o'clock I tried to reach out mentally to see if I could sense anyone. I received absolutely no impressions at all.

After 10 minutes I gave up.

Thanks a lot, Keith. What a load of rubbish. There I was, waiting for my dead fetal brother to contact me in the middle of the night. I was definitely losing it. I got up, yawned and went to bed.

It had been one crazy day.

2

What Do You Do with All That Blue?

What Keith had told me was intriguing, but, as usual, one routine event ran into another like an unending freeway pile-up. Involved in the ordinary mess of life, I forgot about anything else. A two-week summer vacation in Austria was great, but I was worried about Joshua's GCSE exam results. They were due out a couple of weeks after our return to London. These exams are very important in England, similar to high school graduation exams in the U.S. Taken at age 16, their results dictate what higher subjects students can go on to study, and I was worried about Joshua's grades. There was also my ever-present, deteriorating relationship with my parents and sister. I had enough to worry about. Our vacation felt like ancient history after only a few days back home. Life was as hectic as ever and, thankfully, there were no more peculiar consultations.

Then one night, soon after our return, I had a very vivid dream. I often dream, usually in color. Mostly it's pretty meaningless. This dream was different.

It started reasonably enough in my aunt's grand old house. In my dream, my family and I were gathered around her very long dining table enjoying one of her frequent and lavish dinner parties. Draped over the table was a crisp, white, starched tablecloth. Sitting opposite me, across the table, was my cousin. She's a psychotherapist and, for some bizarre reason that seems logical only in dreams, she was trying to get me to organize a chest X-ray for one of her clients. I didn't think it was necessary and was explaining to her why I couldn't arrange it.

Then I became aware of a very short, stocky, dark-skinned Indian-looking man to my left. He was sitting at one end of the table with his back to a wall. On the wall, just above his head, was a light fitting. He appeared to be wearing a flat cap, the sort that, in the north of England, at least, usually goes with a pint of beer and a small dog.

In my dream I heard myself saying, to no one in particular, "I'm not psychic and I can't see auras."

"Of course you can, boss," said the Indian-looking man. Incongruously, he had a Cockney accent. "I'll show you."

With that, he turned and flicked a switch on the wall behind him. The light above his head lit up. But it didn't emit a normal kind of yellow electric light. Instead, all the colors of the rainbow flooded out. The radiating colors completely entranced me. They appeared almost as if they were solid, gem-like shafts of light. There was one predominant color—a clear sky blue.

He then asked me, "What do you do with all that blue?"

As he said this, it was obvious to me what I did with it, as if I'd always known but just temporarily forgotten.

I heard myself saying, "I give it to people," and then experienced an overwhelming flood of emotions. It was a sort of mixture of happiness and wistful sadness so intense I couldn't contain it.

I woke up, crying profusely. I'd never before experienced such a moving dream. It was still very clear in my mind and I felt compelled to wake Punam up: I needed to discuss this.

Punam, as calm as ever, listened to me and didn't dismiss it.

"Do you think I'm going insane?"

She snuggled up to me. "You've always been a little crazy but nothing certifiable."

"Maybe this is my midlife crisis."

Her voice was thick with sleep. "Don't worry. I'll still love you, whatever."

If I was journeying into the Twilight Zone, then clearly I wasn't going to be on my own.

Punam went back to sleep quickly. I lay next to her listening to her breathing, but sleep wouldn't come easily to me. My mind was full of questions. Who was this little Indian-looking guy supposed to be? It seemed he was trying to remind me of something I'd forgotten. I was trying to convince him I wasn't psychic, but he clearly thought otherwise. What was this beautiful blue color I was supposed to be giving to people? And what on earth was all this rubbish about auras?

My rational, scientific side told me it was just a dream. Perhaps Keith's spirit nonsense had unsettled me. With all the stuff that was happening in my life, maybe it wasn't surprising I was having odd dreams. I tried to put it to the back of my mind; after all, there was always something more pressing to think about. I rolled over onto my side and eventually got back to sleep. This time there were no more funny dreams.

3

The Stolen Key

It was the third Thursday in August 2003, and Joshua's school was releasing its students' GCSE exam results that day. I was anxious to finish my morning clinic, do whatever house calls were necessary, and get back home for lunch to see how Joshua had done. I got into the clinic early and took the opportunity to look at the house calls that had been requested so far. When patients phone in to ask for a house call, the receptionist who takes the call writes the details on a page in the house call request book. The doctors then decide which patients they'll see and cross those names off the page.

The book showed we'd received only one house call request that morning. The patient lived within walking distance from the clinic. I wouldn't even have to take my car. If I was fast, I could do the visit before my morning clinic started, which would save time later.

I took the patient's medical notes and went back into my office to get my medical bag. As I wasn't driving, I wouldn't need my keys. I unclipped them from my belt loop and threw them onto my desk. As I stood up to leave the room, I experienced a strange sensation at the back of my head. It felt almost like a slap. It wasn't really a physical impression, though, but definitely felt as if it had come from behind.

"Pick up your keys or they'll get stolen," came unbidden into my mind. I could almost, but not quite, hear the words.

I was already walking out through the door as I dismissed the thought. Nonsense! I always left my keys on my desk. And I was in a real hurry. If I could just get this house call out of the way, I could get home as soon as I'd seen my last booked patient.

Because I was rushing, I went to the wrong house. Stupid! Never mind, the right house was in a parallel street. But because of my initial error, the visit took longer than I'd expected. I arrived back at the clinic with seconds to spare before my first patient arrived.

As I entered the medical center, Anne looked up from the large reception desk.

"Ian, the blue Corsa in the parking lot—is it yours?"

"Yes. Why?"

"Well, we just chased two boys out of it but we think they ran off with your key."

I groaned. "Oh, I just knew that was going to happen! I remember thinking that when I left my keys on my desk."

"So why the bleedin' hell didn't you take them with you, then?" she asked.

"Dunno. Oh, no! I had all my keys on that key ring."

I dashed into my room. Fortunately, the boys had only taken the car key. They'd left my house and clinic keys behind on the desk.

One of our patients who lived in the apartments opposite the medical center had witnessed what had happened. She'd seen two suspicious-looking teenage boys standing in the medical center's parking lot. They'd been pressing the remote unlock button on my key, looking to see which car flashed its indicators. She had telephoned Bel, our manager, who, together with Anne, had rushed into the parking lot. By then the boys were in my car, trying to start it. But it seemed the automatic transmission had foxed them. Caught by surprise, the boys had bolted, but they'd taken the key and locked the car behind them.

I now had a clinic full of patients to see and a locked car I couldn't get into, with no way of knowing what might have been stolen from it. Then the phone rang. It was Joshua. He'd just received his exam results.

He was excited. "Dad I did really well." He told me his grades.

I tried to keep calm. "Oh, well done, Josh!" Then, losing my composure, I said, "They tried to take my car. I've got to go."

Later on, Joshua told me he'd been standing next to his school principal when he'd phoned me. She'd asked him what I'd said.

"Something about his car," he'd told her.

Joshua thought she'd given him a rather pitying look.

So, what do you do when someone runs off with your car keys? Well, first, you phone your spouse, if you're lucky enough to have one who can come around with a spare key. Next, you phone your insurance company. My insurance company told me I needed a crime reference number from the police. Once I had this, they would issue authority to pay for someone to change all of the car's locks.

"All the locks?" I asked.

"Yes, all of them," said the woman on the insurance company's telephone helpline. "That's doors, trunk, and steering lock."

Great. I was really wishing I'd listened to that voice now.

I didn't cancel my clinic. In between patients, I was trying to get through to the local police station to get my crime reference number. But they weren't answering the phone.

Anne sniffed. "Lucky no one's been shot."

She didn't like the police very much.

Ponders End police station (or "nick," as it was known by a few of my less law-abiding patients) was just across the road from the medical center. I'd last paid it a visit about five years before, when someone had stolen a CD containing a copy of

Microsoft Office from my room and I'd had to report it. Then, it had been a spartan, unwelcoming sort of place. You had to press a button to open the main door. A CCTV camera like a Dalek's eyestalk regarded you, and, if it liked you, the door would open with a high-pitched, loud buzz. You'd have to do the same again at another door. Once through this vestibule, you'd be confronted by a large, threatening-looking police officer stationed behind a tall, glass-screened reception counter. Not a nice place. But, as the police still weren't answering the phone, I had little choice but to go there and report the theft in person.

The security at Ponders End nick had been downgraded. The Dalek's eyestalk was still there, but the front door was open, as was the inner door. The reception counter was minus its glass screen. There was no burly policeman, either, as far as I could tell. There was one guy sitting at a desk, which was set back behind, and a little away from, the counter. He was wearing a navy-blue sweater which had a logo patch stitched over its left breast. The patch indicated he worked for the Metropolitan Police in a civilian capacity. With his slight build and delicate features, he really looked quite gentle. A demure, oriental-looking young woman sat next to him. They were both peering at a computer screen, which was sitting on the desk in front of them. There was a man already waiting in front of the counter, so I formed a little queue and took my place behind him.

Drawings and paintings festooned the wall to the left of the counter, softening what had previously been a very austere decor (retro-style, circa 1970s police TV series). Some of them looked like children's Christmas drawings: angels, stars, and so on. Others were really quite good. They all seemed to have a religious theme to them but not exclusively relating to any one particular religion. The pictures seemed to represent imagery from many faiths; there were Buddhist, Hindu, Christian, Moslem, Jewish, and Sikh religious symbols. On the reception counter was a large brass Hindu OM symbol. Next to this was a row of three little Buddha figurines.

I felt slightly disoriented. This wasn't the hard-edged Ponders End nick I remembered. To add to my unease, the man in front of me was taking rather a long time. Even worse, I realized he was one of my patients. He had bad bruising to his face.

He turned, recognized me and said, "Look what the bastards did to me, Doc."

He'd been involved in a fistfight, he told me. Not his fault of course. As I was here, what did I think of the damage? He took off his tee shirt and showed me the bruises on his chest and back. There were many. I smiled weakly. I still didn't have my crime reference number and things were getting mightily surreal. I gritted my teeth.

Eventually, it was my turn. I had to give my details to the civilian police official. He explained they were just upgrading the computer system; it would be a little slow (groan) but once it had my details I would get my crime reference number (hooray). I made a mental effort to relax.

"Ah! It's ready," he said, looking at his computer screen. He glanced up at me. He had very calm-looking, brown eyes.

"Please tell me your date of birth."

I told him.

He gave me a friendly grin. "Oh, so you're a Leo, like me."

"What?" I said, startled.

"I'm also a Leo," he said.

"Oh, are you into astrology, then?" I tried to sound politely interested. What I really wanted to do was grab him around the neck and scream into his face, "JUST GIVE ME MY CRIME REFERENCE NUMBER," but, of course, you just can't do that sort of thing. Especially not in a police station.

Completely ignoring the contents of my consciousness, he explained he'd originally trained as a psychiatric nurse at the local hospital. He'd left nursing to do a degree in comparative spirituality. He was working part-time at the police station in order to fund his studies. As I later learned from my police officer acquaintances, his name was Carl. His colleagues liked him well enough but thought he was completely crazy, though harmless. He offered big macho coppers things like Reiki and spiritual healing after a particularly stressful spell of duty. From my experience of police officers, I suspected this was likely to be a case of pearls before swine. The only spirits they were interested in generally lived in bottles.

"Oh," I said. "If you like all this New Age stuff then you may be interested in this: I think I knew my car was going to be broken into before it happened."

"Really?" Carl slapped the palm of one hand on his desk and nodded furiously. "We were obviously meant to meet!"

He stood up and took something out of a drawer in his desk. It was a pack of cards. Not ordinary cards, though.

He continued talking. "And if we were meant to meet, then I am meant to give you a reading."

He came over to the counter and showed me the cards. They were North American Indian Medicine Cards. I'd never heard of them, but then, hey, I was back in the Twilight Zone! That explained everything.

Carl gave me the pack. "Just shuffle the cards and give them back to me when you've finished."

I did as he asked. He spread the shuffled pack face down on the counter.

"What next?" I asked.

"Now, think of a question in your mind and choose whichever card you feel drawn to."

Sometimes the English language just doesn't have enough words to adequately express one's confusion. Then my mind cleared and a question popped into my head.

I'd spent my spare time over the previous seven years writing a computer program to schedule on-call shifts for doctors and nurses. It had taken up a lot of my time and I'd had some success. I'd even sold one copy to the UK Transplant Authority where it was used to roster their IT support staff. So I asked the cards: Is my software going to be successful?

What the hell, I thought, and selected a card. I turned it over. On it were the words: The world is not yet ready

That's a bugger then, I thought. Seven years of hard work and the world still wasn't ready...

"Can I have my crime reference number now, please?"

I left the police station shaking my head. I felt that if I were to go back there, the door would be locked, I would have to press a buzzer to get back in, and no one would ever have heard of Carl. Perhaps it would be better not to pursue that thought.

When I told my receptionists what had happened, they all started making woo-woo noises and Anne started whistling the Twilight Zone theme.

It took a week to get the car business sorted out.

4

They Obviously Want to Work With You

It was a blazing hot Saturday, two days after my car ordeal. I was standing in the large yard of a huge modern house in Sevenoaks. I'm still not quite sure how I'm related to Victoria, but she'd invited us to a party to meet some relatives who'd come over from the United States. I knew lots of people there, but many only vaguely.

Punam and I got into a conversation with an intense young woman who worked as an occupational therapist. I don't remember how the topic was raised, but she mentioned she'd grown up in a haunted house. I told her about my recent odd experiences, and before I knew it she was telling me about the unusual poltergeist phenomena she and her brother had witnessed as children. This was all very interesting, but my head was starting to fill up and I imagined I could hear the Twilight Zone theme playing again.

I left Punam and the spooky occupational therapist talking together in the yard and retreated into the house.

Inevitably, I ended up in the kitchen. It was crowded with people noisily helping themselves to drinks and food. At the far end of the kitchen, open patio doors framed another, smaller yard. To get away from the throng, I threaded my way through the press of people and headed for the patio doors.

I stepped into what was a more secluded yard. It was empty, save for a man and a woman sitting side by side on a swing bench. The woman was darkly complexioned with black curly hair, a sharp nose, and gray eyes. It was my distant cousin, Rose. She was talking to a younger, plump, fair-haired man.

I overheard her saying, "I used to be a spiritual healer, but I had to give it up when the kids were born."

I just couldn't seem to get away from it today.

The fair-haired man stood up and left to get another glass of wine. I sat down next to Rose.

She smiled at me and asked me why I looked so taken aback. I told her about the strange things that had happened to me recently.

"What do you make of it all, then?" I asked.

"Oh, that's easy." Rose waved a hand dismissively. Then she pointed at me. "They obviously want to work with you."

"Who do?"

"The spirits. This is how it starts. Don't worry about it. You'll get used to all these things happening. You're on the path."

I took a swig of Pimm's from my glass. "Hmm. I'm either on some sort of path or being led up the garden path."

I swirled my drink around the glass, idly watching bubbles rising from a piece of cucumber as the liquid settled. "How do you think they want to work with me, then?"

"Well, maybe they want to help you with your work."

"In what way?"

"As a doctor, you'd already have healing guides working with you. They've been helping you without you knowing it."

"Is that so?" I did my best to sound skeptical.

This was all news to me. Primary care physicians in the UK half-jokingly talk about the three-way consultation: the physician, the patient, and the computer. Surely my office couldn't get any more crowded?

"How would they be helping me?"

"Oh, you know, maybe by inspiring you with ideas; possibly by allowing healing energy to flow through you. That would explain the blue energy you give to people. Blue is the color of healing."

I had no idea how Rose could possibly think healing had a color. How could any activity have a color? But as far as she was concerned, it was all quite simple—way too simple for a scientifically educated doctor like me.

"Rose, forgive me, but this all sounds like a very medieval way of looking at the world—everything down to spirits and so on. I mean, why would they be doing this? Don't these spirits have anything else to do?"

Rose shrugged her shoulders.

"I don't know. I suppose they've got lots of things to do. But, after all, they're only human. If they used to be doctors or nurses when they were alive, then many of them will still want to help people on our side of life. But they need someone to work through."

I thought about this.

"Hmm. Now that you mention it, an odd thing happened to me a couple of years ago."

I told Rose what had happened.

I'd introduced myself to Catherine one day while I was training in the gym. I'd overheard her telling someone she had a phobia about driving. She could only drive her car when her husband was with her. I had a strong feeling I could help her using hypnosis. We didn't know each other then but I explained I was a local physician. I told her I was sure I could help her if she came to see me in my clinic. I wouldn't normally make such a suggestion to a complete stranger who wasn't my patient, but for some reason I felt moved to make the offer.

Catherine proved to be a good hypnotic subject and very quickly became a confident driver. This was just as well because within a few months her mother, who lived in Hastings, developed Parkinson's disease. Fortunately, Catherine was now able to drive herself to Hastings to visit her. We became friendly and, if we saw each other in the gym, we'd work out together and have a chat.

I usually only go to the gym during my weekday lunch break. However, one Saturday morning I felt very edgy and unable to relax. The feeling I had was similar to the sort of electrical build-up you sometimes get before a thunderstorm. In fact, I felt compelled to go to the gym.

Punam told me to go and work it off, as I was getting on her nerves.

I found Catherine working out in the gym and we got talking. She mentioned that her granddaughter, Kirsty, had swallowed the cap from a plastic ballpoint pen while at school the previous day.

"And what did the school do?" I asked.

"They gave her a drink of water and it went down," she said.

With that, I had an awful, pressing feeling in my chest. As I experienced this, I developed a strong impression she'd inhaled the pen cap and it had lodged in one of the main tubes of her lungs. It would usually be obvious and very distressing to anyone who'd done this. However, in this case I somehow knew Kirsty hadn't realized what had happened to her.

"How is she now?" I asked.

"She's fine. Why? Do you think something's wrong?"

I could tell I'd started to worry Catherine, but something was telling me Kirsty was in danger.

"Cathy, I think you ought to phone and find out how Kirsty is." I pointed to her cell phone, which was on the floor next to her locker key.

Catherine picked up the phone and speed-dialed Vicky, her daughter. She spoke briefly, then handed me the phone.

"Vicky, you don't know me, but I'm one of your mother's friends and I'm a doctor. She told me Kirsty swallowed part of a pen yesterday. How is she?"

"Oh. Hello. She seems fine."

"Is she completely normal? Are you sure?"

"Well, yes...apart from the fact that she didn't feel like going to her ballet lesson last night."

"Vicky, is she breathing normally?"

"Yes."

"No wheezing?"

"No. I'd know if she was because I used to suffer from a bit of asthma myself when I was younger."

"Look...just humor me for a moment. Ask her to run around the yard a few times to get her breathing going a bit faster."

Vicky did as instructed.

"How's Kirsty now?" I asked.

"Er...actually, she's a bit wheezy." Now Vicky sounded worried.

"Can you put your ear to the back of her chest while she's wheezing and listen to each side in turn? Is the wheezing more on one side than the other?"

Again, she did as I asked.

"I think it's coming from the right side of her chest. But now she's stopped breathing heavily, I can't hear it," she said, after about 30 seconds.

As far I was concerned, that clinched it. Inhaled objects usually travel down the main tube of the right lung—the right main bronchus. I was now convinced Kirsty had an inhaled foreign body lodged in her right main bronchus.

I telephoned the pediatrician who was on call at the local hospital. I arranged for Kirsty to be seen, even though she wasn't my patient and I hadn't even seen her or examined her. I'd never done anything like this before.

Catherine went off very upset. She was convinced I was

right. Once she left, I became worried that I'd behaved very foolishly. After all, I knew I was just an ordinary doctor; I was never going to be God's gift to medicine. Suppose I was wrong.

I found out the following Monday what had happened at the hospital.

The pediatric team had examined her and pronounced her fit and well. Kirsty had behaved normally and they'd allowed her to go home. Meanwhile, Catherine and Vicky were in a very anxious state, not knowing what to believe. The next morning, they went back to the hospital and explained how worried they were. Very sensibly, the pediatric resident who was on-call that Sunday contacted the Hospital for Sick Children in Great Ormond Street. He didn't think there was anything wrong. However, faced with a worried grandmother and mother, he felt obliged to seek a second opinion.

Kirsty had her chest X-rayed at Great Ormond Street Hospital. The X-ray was normal and, again, the doctor there told Catherine and Vicky not to worry. Nevertheless, they were both adamant that Kirsty should have more tests. Obviously, I'd really spooked them.

The doctor told them the only way to be one hundred percent sure was to use a bronchoscope, a tube that's pushed down the windpipe in order to look into the lungs. However, he didn't recommend it; Kirsty would need an anesthetic and it was quite a big thing to put a child through.

By this time, Catherine and Vicky were frantic and insisted that Kirsty should have the bronchoscope examination.

That afternoon, the doctor looking after Kirsty extracted the chewed cap of a red plastic ballpoint pen from her right main bronchus. Because she'd chewed it, the plastic cap had frayed into little barbs so that it had begun to embed itself into the wall of the bronchus. It was unlikely she would have been able to cough it up. The consequences of it being left in her lung for any length of time would have been disastrous for Kirsty's health. She would have developed pneumonia or possibly even a serious chronic lung condition called bronchiectasis.

Rose listened to my story with interest.

When I finished telling it, she said, "Ian, you're definitely on the path. It looks like they've been working with you for some time."

I thought about it and realized just how strange the whole episode had been. I'd always wondered how I'd made that diagnosis.

"So, if they're already working with me, why is all this weird stuff happening to me all of a sudden? Why not just carry on as before?"

Rose paused in thought for a few moments and then said, "I suppose they're hoping that once you realize they want to work with you, you can make it easier for them to get through. After all, communication should be a two-way process."

"But how can I be sure they want to work with me? It all seems so unlikely."

"I think it's already started. Watch out for coincidences. That's how you know they're working. Like with Catherine."

I tried to grasp what she was telling me. I could see that from her point of view it might make some sense. But I just wasn't comfortable with the idea.

I tried to make light of my confusion. I stood up. "Rose, you're doing my head in and I think I need another drink. Do you want one?"

She shook her head.

"Just make sure you look out for those coincidences!" she said, as I left.

I turned, raised my empty glass, and smiled. Of course, once someone tells you to start looking out for coincidences you start to see them everywhere. I didn't have to wait long.

5

I've Got an Alien Living in My Apartment

The week after the party in Sevenoaks, I noticed that the latest edition of *Pulse* medical magazine featured the first ever review of computer software for managing on-call duty rosters. This was exactly what the software I'd been developing was designed to do. Maybe my seven years of hard work was about to be recognized! I excitedly opened the magazine and leafed through the pages to find the article. It didn't mention my software. As Carl's North American Indian Medicine Cards had said in the police station, the world was not yet ready. Indeed the world may never be ready.

With a mental sigh of disappointment, I was just about to place my copy of *Pulse* in the doctors' magazine rack when another article caught my eye. On the same page as the software review was a smaller article about a physician who was also a spiritual healer. Apparently, he'd become a healer after experiencing a number of strange occurrences. He now both practiced and taught spiritual healing. Any interested doctors could contact him via email.

So, here were two things that had been occupying my mind recently—duty roster software and weirdness, specifically spiritual weirdness. Both had turned up on the same page of the magazine I usually read. And I'd just been warned to watch out for coincidences. Could this be one of them? I had to find out. I emailed the physician mentioned in the magazine article, explaining what had been happening to me. What on earth did he make of it all?

I received a one-line email back. It was his telephone number followed by: "Phone me this evening. We need to talk."

"What do you think I should do?" I asked Punam that evening.

"Phone him. What have you got to lose?"

"My sanity? Hmm. Too late. Why not phone him, then?"

We had a brief conversation. He spoke in a quiet monotone, as if he were fearful someone might be listening, someone just over his shoulder.

"If this is happening to you, then they definitely want to work with you," he said.

"Do you honestly think my patient can see spirits?"

"Oh, yes. Why not? I see spirit all the time. There's a whole unseen universe out there. Once you tune in, you realize just what you've been missing. I've even got an alien living in my apartment. He's quite shy, but I know he's there."

Was this how it ended, in an apartment somewhere looking for aliens? I made a neutral "uh-huh" remark, just to let him know I was listening and that, well, you know, who doesn't have an alien living in their apartment nowadays!

"Of course, you have to find out how they want to work with you," he continued.

"How do you mean?" I asked.

"Well, it all overlaps, of course, but some tend more towards healing and others more towards mediumship. Or you can do both. I'm sure you'll be shown the way."

I vaguely remembered an article about healing I'd read a couple of years before. It had been in the *British Medical Journal*. A physician who was also a healer had written a very sensible and well-balanced account of her experiences. No aliens. Hardly Twilight Zone stuff at all. I already had some expertise in hypnosis and acupuncture. Maybe healing would be another string to my bow.

"So, how exactly does one become a healer, then?" I asked.

"There's a formal training program. You need to do the

training in order to be recognized. It takes two years, even if you're medically qualified. It's just a piece of paper at the end of the day, but these things do count."

He mentioned the National Federation of Spiritual Healers and gave me the telephone number of someone who could help me. He said he would send me more information in the mail.

I looked up the National Federation of Spiritual Healers on the internet. They seemed a respectable organization. I decided to phone them—one day.

Two days later, I received a large envelope at the clinic. It was marked "Highly Confidential." Inside this was another, much smaller, envelope. It was also marked "Highly Confidential." Inside this was a poorly produced pamphlet for the course on healing that the "I've-got-an-alien-living-in-my-apartment" doctor was running. Appropriately enough, the course was in the famous hippy heartland town of Glastonbury.

I assumed he was trying to save me any embarrassment were my secretary to open the letter. Fat chance of that! By then the receptionists and secretaries were hanging on my every word.

"Hello, Ian. Any more coincidences?"

"Had any more Spiritualist readings then, Ian?"

I told them I was probably having one of those flamboyant midlife crises sometimes experienced by men of a certain age. It could have been worse—I could have bought a sports car.

However, suppose all this stuff wasn't just in my head. At the risk of having a mind so open that my brain would drop out, I was beginning to accept the possibility that spirits really existed, or at least, that paranormal phenomena were real. I'd started to read extensively around the subject. Despite all the dross, there did seem to be a few gold nuggets. Maybe there was a case to be made for it.

Then again, maybe not. Perhaps my patient Keith Bishop had just made a few lucky guesses and led me on. And, after all, if I left my car keys on my desk when my room was empty, I was simply asking for trouble. The rational part of my mind was trying to prop up my existing worldview.

I needed more evidence if I was going to take this seriously. This had now become personal and it was beginning to worry me. So, had I any more personal evidence? In fact, on reflection, over the years I'd had quite a bit. It was just that—well, I'd kind of filed it away in the back of my mind.

6

Personal Evidence

Work, raising a family, and generally muddling through life tends to keep our thoughts focused on normal, everyday things. When something strange occurs, it's very hard to know what to do with it. The effort of trying to understand how unusual experiences fit into our lives is just too great. So we simply don't bother. If we ever recall what happened, maybe when something jogs our memory, then perhaps we mention it as an interesting story. Otherwise we ignore it and get stuck back into our everyday, normal lives.

That's pretty much the way I'd handled it. But maybe now the time had come to take these experiences out of my mental filing cabinet and see how they fit together.

Water in the Light

My first odd experience occurred when I was 16, in 1971. At the time, I lived in Tottenham in north London in a large, semi-detached Victorian house.

There were eight of us that Saturday night. It had been raining hard so we'd closed the living room windows. Eight 16-year-olds regarded the glass-topped living room table with an unlikely interest. We'd arranged Scrabble letters in a rough circle on the table, spelling out the letters of the alphabet. In the middle of the spread was a glass tumbler, turned upside-down. In a corner of the room an old Dansette mono record player was thrashing out a space-rock number by Hawkwind.

"Okay," I said. "We all put one finger on the glass and ask a question."

"Who's gonna ask?" queried Pete, who looked at the glass

with something approaching reverence.

Unlike the rest of us, Pete wasn't going into senior year. That summer he would leave school to join the Royal Navy where he'd be billeted with a contingent of lads from Cornwall. Within two weeks he'd be speaking with a broad Cornish accent. Pete, never the brightest, was very impressionable.

"Would you like to do it, Pete?" asked Ralph, the natural leader of our little group.

"Yeah." Pete nodded furiously.

"You should say, 'Spirit of the glass, are you there?'" I recommended.

Pete furrowed his brow in concentration. "Spirit of the glass, are you there? Right." He nodded again, this time more slowly, more thoughtfully.

"Let's start, then." I turned off the lights.

We had no candles. Instead, I'd set up the butane canister Bunsen burner from my chemistry set. It sat at one end of the table, its flame adjusted to a softly flickering yellow. I lifted the playing-arm of the Dansette. In the sudden silence, we could hear the rain beating on the window. The Bunsen burner, the warm, humid weather, and the eight of us made the room stiflingly hot.

We all knew what to do. Who didn't? The Ouija board was one of the most popular diversions among teenagers in those days. Not that we'd ever got much out of it ourselves. But we'd all heard stories of the glass taking on a life of its own, perhaps even smashing to smithereens or spelling out some frightening message. At the very least, it gave us all something to do whenever we met at my place. It made a change from sitting in the dark at Ralph's house. Most Saturday evenings we'd go there to listen to his extensive rock music collection. We'd sip homemade, too-sweet wine until his father came home from the Tottenham Liberal and Radical social club, drunk and spoiling for a fight with his Irish neighbors.

I had no stereo, and the records were courtesy of whoever decided to bring whatever music they fancied that evening. I had no sweet wine to offer either, just instant coffee.

I'd grown up in a family that only ever talked about politics. But I wanted to know about more than just power in the political sense. I had a burning interest in science and anything to do with the unconscious mind. The year before, I'd taught myself hypnosis. From being inconspicuous, bespectacled, and geeky, I'd inadvertently transformed myself into the most sought-after person at school by the neat trick of hypnotizing Alan Stockwell. Hippy-haired, acid-tripping Alan was good-looking and very popular. He'd introduced me to some interesting books. In return, I'd shown him how he could trip without acid, using just his mind and self-hypnosis. Word got around. I experimented on my school friends and became aware of just how powerful the unconscious mind can be. In fact, it had all got a little bit out of hand. I had people queuing, waiting outside the school library for me to hypnotize them.

In the end, the principal called me into her office and asked me, very nicely, to stop doing it.

"I have a degree in psychology, Ian, and I do believe in hypnosis. But it isn't really appropriate to do it at school," she said.

I agreed to stop hypnotizing my fellow students on school premises. She made me sign a neatly typed letter on school stationery, which said that after discussion with the school authorities I'd agreed to stop. I was too young to realize she was just covering her ass with paperwork. That was in the 1960s. Of course, we're all doing it now. I guess she must have been ahead of her time.

But all of a sudden, I had friends. I learned to join in and got interested in rock music. I couldn't do any more far-out experiments at school, but in my house we did what I wanted. And what I wanted most was to see what we could get from the Ouija board. There was a theory that the glass responded to the unconscious mind, and I wanted to test it out.

We each placed one finger on the glass...and instantly started giggling.

Pete got upset. This was *his* moment. "Shut up. Shut up," he hissed.

We calmed down and waited for the glass to move. Slowly, it started to slide over the glass tabletop, occasionally making a squealing glass-on-glass noise until it picked up speed.

Very seriously, Pete leaned forward and said, "Spirit of the glass, are you there?"

The glass stopped, as if it were listening. Pete leaned forward even further. "Spirit of the glass, are you there?"

The glass jerked a couple of times and then glided more smoothly across the table. It slowly indicated the letters YES.

Pete looked at me triumphantly. "You see, it's there!"

"Ask it for a message," suggested Ralph.

Pete asked the glass for a message. We all giggled at how earnest he was. He clearly had no doubts. As far as he was concerned, there genuinely was a spirit moving the glass. After a while, the glass started to move again.

It spelled out WATER.

"What do you mean, Spirit?" asked Pete. By now, he was talking to the glass as if it were an old friend.

"Maybe it wants a drink?" someone said, facetiously.

"Don't be stupid," said Pete, now completely absorbed. "Spirits don't need to drink." Then, addressing the glass, he asked, "Spirit, what do you mean?"

The glass started to move again. We all winced as it squealed over the glass tabletop.

Next, it spelled out DANGER. Ooh! This was more like it.

"If it tells us someone's gonna die, we stop," said Ralph, firmly. We all murmured in agreement.

The glass picked up speed.

WATER WATER.

"Okay," said Richard. "We've got that. Tell us some more."

LIGHT.

Someone gave a mock yawn. The room was warm and stuffy, and what we were getting wasn't making any sense.

"Keep going," said Ralph. "Let's see if we get anything else." He fixed his gaze on the glass and said, "We don't understand." His tone was impatient.

The glass didn't move.

Pete gave Ralph a reproachful look and then said, respectfully, "Spirit of the glass. We don't understand you. Can you give us some more?"

To his delight, the glass started to move again. "Thank you, Spirit," he said and smirked at Ralph. Ralph flicked his long straight hair back, sniffed, and raised his eyes to heaven.

WATER LIGHT DANGER.

We debated what the words could mean. We couldn't understand what the Ouija board was trying to tell us, and we were beginning to get bored. We tried again. Finally, it spelled out:

WATER IN THE LIGHT DANGER.

We still didn't understand but decided to try it one last time.

WATER IN THE LIGHT DANGER.

We were stumped.

"What a load of rubbish," said Richard.

"Not good," agreed John.

"Okay," I said. "Let's stop."

I turned on the lights and turned off the Bunsen burner.

Pete looked sad. "Goodbye, Spirit," he said.

The rest of us groaned and someone flicked a Scrabble letter at him.

"I'll make coffee," I said.

I left the living room. It was slightly less muggy in the hallway. The rain had stopped. I walked down the hall into the kitchen and turned on the kitchen light.

The light had a peculiar yellowish cast to it. There was something wrong. I looked up at the light and yelled out. The opaque glass goldfish bowl lampshade was half-full of water.

Everyone came running into the kitchen and just stood there looking up at the light in amazement.

WATER IN THE LIGHT DANGER. The glass had spoken the truth.

My father worked out what had happened when he came home later that evening. The bathroom was above the kitchen. The bathroom window had been left open. The rain had been so heavy it had blown in through the window, and rainwater had run down the wall and soaked the floor. Water had seeped through the floorboards and found its way through the electrical wiring into the kitchen ceiling.

I'd been the first person to leave the room that evening since it had started raining. No one could possibly have known what had happened before I'd left the room. We were all dead impressed.

My second unusual event occurred that same year. However, at the time I didn't think much of it. It took a couple of years before I realized its true significance.

A Name Like Pam

In those days, there weren't many Indians in my school.

Other than Sharmeelee Shah, I hadn't met any and I knew nothing about Indian culture. My friend Steve really liked Sharmeelee. I liked Laura who was pretty and blonde and I really couldn't understand what Steve saw in Sharmeelee.

I was at home one winter's evening. I was just about to walk downstairs from my bedroom. The kerosene heater was glowing brightly on the landing below, and I can still remember its vaporous smell. I was idly wondering why Steve liked Sharmeelee so much. I suddenly experienced a strange physical sensation, almost as if a cloak had been placed over my shoulders and something like a hood had been pulled up to cover the back of my head. With this sensation came the knowledge that I was going to marry an Indian girl with a name like Pam. I felt as if the information had come from behind me, almost as if the hooded cloak sensation had somehow put the information into the back of my mind. I clearly remember thinking to myself that I couldn't contemplate such a thing, that I wanted to marry Laura, and anyway I didn't know any Indians named Pam.

I went to Nottingham medical school in 1973. Punam and I were in the same study group at medical school and we got along well enough. But I didn't get the chance to know her better that first term because she lived off-campus with her parents and went home every evening.

We got together in January 1974, at Maggie's birthday party, at the beginning of the second term. Even then, I didn't realize she was Indian. With her fair complexion, she reminded me of a Turkish girl I'd known at school. I eventually found out she'd been born in Delhi, India. She'd come to England when she was four years old. If you remove the letters U and N from her name, you end up with PAM. Of course, we did eventually marry.

But the incident with the highest strangeness factor was yet to come.

Felicity's Face

If I were allowed to tell you only one story, it would have to be this.

It was now August 1974. I was 19 years old. All my school friends who'd gone away to university were back in London for summer vacation. My close friend Nick, who'd gone to Leicester University to study physics, had brought his new girlfriend, Felicity, back to London to stay for a few weeks.

One evening Felicity, my sister (then aged 15), and I had been having an ordinary conversation in Nick's living room. It was quite late, perhaps ten or eleven o'clock at night. The tone changed when Nick, who'd been in the kitchen, strode into the room determined to tell a creepy story. He clapped his hands together and said, "Right!"

As he did so, we all felt something strange. There was a sensation of "green-ness" about the place, as if the quality of the light in the room had changed. We all felt it and commented upon it. It gradually faded and he told his story, which ended with him making my sister jump with fright. We all laughed at her reaction. The atmosphere returned to normal and we fell to ordinary conversation. We'd been chatting for perhaps another five minutes.

Nick and Felicity were sitting side by side on a sofa opposite me. Nick was to the left of Felicity. My sister was sitting in an easy chair to my right, where she could clearly see our profiles.

Felicity was pretty, with waist-long dark hair, dark eyes, and a slightly ruddy complexion. Although she was going out with Nick, I knew she liked me as well, and I'd been stringing her along, flattered by the attention she'd been paying me.

I was speaking and happened to glance at her. But instead

of Felicity, I found myself staring at a snow queen—a female entity with shoulder-length blonde hair and well-defined cheekbones. In particular, she had inhumanly thick lips, as if they were somehow distorted, which appeared very pale, as if she was wearing frosted lipstick. Her ice-blue eyes were the most striking thing about her. She was looking at me—or rather, she was looking through me, into my soul. It was as if her eyes were radiating a pure white, penetrating light. Her look was very stern, yet not unkind. It seemed to convey a number of messages:

Keep back. Leave Felicity alone. Remember what you have seen. Know there is more to life than meets the eye. You will understand one day.

This lasted maybe two or three seconds. Tears were running down my face. I could hear someone screaming. My sister had jumped up out of her chair and was shouting at the top of her voice, "My God, can you see those lips?"

I turned to my sister and said, "What? You've seen it too?"

When I looked again at Felicity, she was completely normal.

Felicity had felt nothing, and Nick was completely bemused. As far as they were concerned, we'd been having an ordinary conversation when I'd started crying and my sister had started screaming.

When we'd finished running around in a panic, we bundled into my car and I drove us all to my house. It was now two o'clock in the morning, and my parents weren't pleased to be woken up by a bunch of hysterical teenagers. They suggested I take Nick and Felicity home.

The next day we told our friends what had happened. My sister confirmed we'd both seen the same thing. However, as she'd seen Felicity's profile, she'd been struck, in particular, by her large, somewhat distorted, and very pale lips. Steve suggested we have a word with his neighbor Keith Hudson.

I'd first met Keith the summer before. I'd just finished my senior high school exams and was about to embark on my medical studies. Keith was then in his late twenties. He was tall and gangly, wore thick glasses, and was beginning to lose his hair. He was an unusual and interesting person, with a passion for old books. Keith also claimed to be a Spiritualist medium.

I remember sitting with Keith in Steve's living room one evening when there was a knock at the street door. It was John, and as he walked into the living room, Keith glanced up at him and said, "You've just had a car accident, haven't you?"

"How on earth did you know that, Keith?" asked John.

Keith grinned, pointed a finger upwards, and said, "They just told me."

That same evening Keith looked at me and said, "You've got a lot of knowledge around you, Ian. You don't know that you know it, but you will one day."

I wasn't much impressed. Having just completed my high school senior year and with university beckoning, I reckoned that was an easy one. Anyone could have said that.

Whatever the truth or otherwise of Keith's psychic powers, we all thought he'd be the best person to explain what had happened to Felicity the night before.

Later that day, at Steve's house, we told Keith what had happened. He was completely unfazed and explained that what we'd witnessed was known as transfiguration. We'd seen Felicity's spirit guide who'd been protecting her, presumably from me, as I'd been toying with her feelings.

After Keith had left, we discussed what he'd said. Either his explanation was correct or somehow my sister and I had shared a hallucination. Both, scientifically speaking, were impossible.

So, I'd had three unusual experiences. Believing I'd somehow been told the name and background of my future wife was a purely personal experience with no supporting evidence from anyone else. It would be easy to dismiss. However, my sister and my friends could corroborate the other two incidents, which were therefore harder to discount.

Now strange things were happening again, I needed to find out how this all fit together.

It's said that when the student is ready, the teacher appears. The last time I'd seen Keith was in 1976, at Steve's wedding, two years before I qualified as a doctor. I had no idea Keith Hudson was about to come back into my life in a big way.

7

More Encompassing Than God

I had to acknowledge that weird events had started happening to me again. What could this mean? Just suppose spirits were real and they wanted to work with me. As my everyday work was in the medical sphere, did this mean they wanted me to explore spiritual healing? Not that I knew much about the subject. Although I'd looked at their website, I hadn't yet contacted the National Federation of Spiritual Healers.

The "I've-got-an-alien-living-in-my-apartment" doctor had given me the phone number of someone at the London Integrated Medicine Association (LIMA). LIMA was a loose affiliation of spiritual healers and conventional doctors who are also interested in spiritual healing. I spoke on the phone to Simon, LIMA's secretary.

He explained that just because I was a doctor, it didn't mean I was destined to become a healer. What I needed was to get a "reading" from a channeler. He knew just the person. But if I *was* interested in seeing what healing involved, I should get in touch with the head of training at my local section of the National Federation of Spiritual Healers.

We exchanged contact details and it turned out Simon lived exactly across my uncle's old apartment. He wondered if it was significant. Now well and truly in the Twilight Zone, I did too. I put the phone down. I had no qualms about contacting the National Federation of Spiritual Healers, but a channeler? I discussed it with Punam. Why not? If nothing else, it would be an interesting experience.

It took me a while to pluck up the courage to book an appointment with the channeler. The woman at the other end of the line was extremely well spoken and business-like. It would cost me 35 pounds, and she was fully booked until well into the following year. She gave me an appointment for a Wednesday afternoon in May 2004. As I put the phone down, I wondered what I'd let myself in for. But it was sufficiently far into the future that I could effectively forget about it for the time being.

My next contact was less difficult for me. Brenda was head of training of the local section of the National Federation of Spiritual Healers. Over the phone, I explained to her I was a doctor who was interested in finding out about spiritual healing. She suggested I come to see what happens at their trainee workshop over in Stanmore. She ran healing sessions on Wednesday evenings for her trainees in Glebe Hall, a local community hall, which used to be a small scout hut, just off Stanmore High Street. Anyone could come along and have healing from a trainee for a nominal sum.

"Make sure you turn left at Glebe Road, immediately before Sainsbury's supermarket," she advised.

It was only a 25-minute drive to Stanmore, on a freezing cold winter's evening. Glebe Hall was a small, single story, creosoted wooden building. It looked like something out of the 1950s but with a New Age makeover. I went inside and was immediately aware of the smell of incense and the sound of tinkling, ethereal music. A gas heater was set against the middle of the wall to the left of the door. It gave off a cheery glow, which made the interior of the hut, little more than a single, large room, comfortably warm. The atmosphere was calm and peaceful. People were paired off together, with each trainee healer standing behind a seated patient. There were about 15 or 16 pairs, and this made the room feel a little crowded. The healers held their arms over their patients but never seemed to touch them.

There was one examination couch in the room. A woman was lying on it, and a young man who looked like a classic Jesus figure (long hair, beard, and robe) stood with his arms spread over her. It looked very impressive.

There was a small group of people sitting quietly together on a couple of settees in one corner of the room. I introduced myself to them and explained I was interested in seeing what spiritual healing was all about. Derek—bald, middle-aged, and bespectacled—had a chat with me.

I mentioned the fact that, as a doctor from a non-practicing Jewish background, I found Spiritualism somewhat difficult to accept.

Derek laughed and said he was also Jewish. "You get all sorts of Spiritualists from all religious backgrounds. There are lots of Jewish Spiritualists and many well-known mediums are also Jewish."

"But according to Judaism, you shouldn't meddle with spirits," I said.

"But it's a mitzvah to heal," he countered. I couldn't argue with that; it certainly is a mitzvah (good deed or divine commandment) to heal, whatever one's religion or lack of it.

So let's see what spiritual healing was all about. He suggested I try it. Did I have any problems I wanted healed? Not particularly.

"Never mind," he said. "Try it, anyway."

He introduced me to one of the trainee healers, a thin, young woman who asked me to sit down on an ordinary upright chair. She stood behind me with her hands on my shoulders. She then slowly swept her hands over my body, limbs, and head in a methodical manner, always keeping a couple of inches away from touching me. I didn't feel anything and I'm not sure it helped much. Nevertheless, with the incense, soft music, and warmth from the gas fire on a cold winter's night, it was a soothing experience.

When my trainee healer had finished, she said to me in a confidential manner, "We aren't meant to say this to patients, but you've got a lovely aura."

I didn't know how to reply, so I just grinned stupidly at her. I suppose I should have asked her what color it was.

I couldn't imagine doing this sort of thing with my patients. It was decidedly too passive for my taste. So, perhaps the spirits didn't want to work with me after all.

One of the great things about being a primary care physician is that you'll always find you attract patients who have the same interests as yourself. Over the years, I've taken up karate, woodworking, and computer programming. And I've had the good fortune to meet martial artists, woodworkers, and computer programmers who were all able to give me some useful tips.

Dave Godfrey was an impressive man in his mid-fifties. Tall and well built, he had long gray hair tied back with beads and feathers. He wore hippy beads around his neck and sported a wizard-like gray beard. An ex-science teacher, he was a relic of the flower power era. Now a practitioner of alternative medicine and wannabe urban shaman, he was a remarkably sensible and solid sort of person. Perhaps this was because his misgivings about Western medicine were tempered by the fact that he was an insulin-dependent diabetic and therefore required complex medication for his health.

Over the years that we'd known each other, Dave had told me about a few of his odd experiences as a healer. I mentioned to him what had been happening to me lately and that I was going to see a channeler.

"You know, Ian," he said. "That's all well and good, but there are some strange people out there. If you really want to get a handle on this, you need to find a psychic development circle." He explained that a psychic development circle or awareness circle is a group of people who meet on a regular basis to explore their psychic gifts.

"The only place you're likely to find one is attached to a Spiritualist church."

I told him I didn't fancy going to anything that called itself a church. It just didn't feel right.

"Well," he said, "you don't have to be religious, but it really is the only way you'll get any sort of control over this."

"Okay," I said, still feeling uncertain. "How do I find a circle to join?"

"That's the problem. There aren't many of them, and most of them are closed, which means you have to be invited to join. You usually have to be a member of a Spiritualist church. Ideally, you want an open circle, which is one where you can just turn up. I haven't the foggiest idea where you'll find one. Mind you, though," Dave looked at me over his reading glasses with a rather stern, schoolteacher-ish look, "if spirit wants to work with you, you'll be shown the way."

"You mean 'spirits,' Dave, don't you?"

"Spirit, Ian. We say 'spirit.' Singular. It's a bit like God, only more encompassing."

One day soon after, Punam was reading the local newspaper. Glancing through the announcements page, her gaze fell on a small box advertising the times of divine services at a local Spiritualist church.

"Ian, what was the name of that Spiritualist medium you used to know?"

"Keith Hudson. That name's a blast from the past. When was the last time I saw him?" It took me a couple of seconds to remember. "I know. Steve's wedding. That's got to be what?

Almost 30 years ago, I guess."

She showed me the newspaper. "It says here he's giving an address at the Beacon of Light Spiritualist Church this Thursday. Why don't we go along?"

What me? A good Jewish boy, go to a church? With my Hindu wife? Okay, then—maybe I wasn't such a good Jewish boy. Maybe I would go there and Keith would give me a message. I bet he wouldn't remember me, though.

As Punam and I sat in the crowded Spiritualist church, I wondered how much Keith had changed over the last three decades. I knew I had. When I was younger, I had a mass of dark curly hair, a beard, and I used to wear contact lenses. Now I had gray hair, where I had any hair at all. Clean-shaven and wearing glasses, older and stockier, I was essentially unrecognizable from the adolescent I'd once been.

I'd never been to a Spiritualist church service before. The church was small and cozy. Opposite the entrance doors was a small, raised platform. To one side of the platform was an upright piano. I looked at the congregation. I'd expected to see many elderly ladies, but to my surprise there were also a quite a few younger women and men as well.

The service started with a prayer and a few hymns, which reminded me of the assemblies we used to have when I was at primary school. After a short address to the congregation and further prayers, Keith Hudson stood up to give clairvoyance. He would try to tune into the spirits, sorry, spirit, and see if he could get any messages for members of the congregation.

I was surprised at how little he'd changed. I could certainly match him up to the person I remembered. He started and then proceeded at a fair clip. One by one, he went to practically every member of the congregation with a short message. He would describe an individual, tell how they'd "passed" and then give a brief message. He even gave one to Punam, which sounded as if it had come from someone remarkably like her grandmother.

When he came to me, all he said was, "Sir, I see you have a lot of knowledge around you. You don't know that you know it, but you will soon. And they are asking me to tell you to write it down."

It was the same message he'd given me when I'd first met him in 1973. I didn't think he recognized me. Even if he did, he certainly wouldn't remember something he'd said to me 30 years before as a throwaway comment. Maybe he said the same thing to everyone. Mind you, he hadn't that evening. He'd only said it to me.

The service finished at half past nine and the president of the congregation stood up and made an announcement. "Can anyone give Mr. Hudson a lift home as he doesn't have a car?"

I put my hand up and shouted, "I'll give Keith a lift. But only if he comes home with me for a cup of tea first!"

I jumped up and walked towards the platform. Plainly, Keith hadn't recognized me because he stepped back a little, obviously nervous at my effusive behavior.

"Keith! It's me! Ian Rubenstein."

Light dawned and his face broke into a huge grin. "Ian? The doctor?"

"Yes!"

"Ian! I was only talking about you the other day!"

I introduced him to Punam.

Later that evening we sat in my kitchen, Keith by the back door, which I'd opened to let out the smoke from his cigarette. I'd yet to realize that mediums tend to be heavy smokers.

"You weren't half surprised to see me," I said.

Keith grinned. "Oh, you do get some headcases at Spiritualist services. It tends to attract them. You've got to be careful."

We chatted about the people we'd both known, most of

whom we'd lost touch with. It had been a long time. Since I'd last seen Keith, he'd left his job as a factory supervisor and started up a couple of bookshops specializing in esoteric literature. He'd finished that venture and now devoted all his time to mediumship and clairvoyance. He was unmarried, still interested in second-hand books, which he collected avidly, and lived in a one-room apartment in Walthamstow. Conveniently close to his apartment, his base now was Vestry Road Spiritualist Church, where he stored his books, took services, and sat on the church committee.

It was a 20-minute journey from my house in Enfield to Walthamstow.

"Tell you what," said Keith. "Why don't you drop me off at my church and I'll show you around."

I hadn't been to Walthamstow for years; my cousins used to live there. When I was very young, I would visit them most weekends as it was only a couple of miles to the east of where I'd grown up in Tottenham. As we drove past the impressive Walthamstow Town Hall with its gushing fountain, I realized I was re-visiting my childhood.

Walthamstow is a busy, bustling borough in northeast London. Once a quiet hamlet east of the River Lee, it's now a run-down inner-city area with old Victorian housing stock. But there's one vestige of that ancient hamlet still left. Known as Walthamstow Village, it's a narrow road boasting magnificent old buildings, a couple of them timber-framed and of Tudor origin, close to St Mary's Church. Opposite St Mary's Church is a low Victorian building, originally a fire station, then a school and now Vestry Road Spiritualist Church. Keith unlocked the side door and showed me around.

"We have an open circle here every Thursday. You don't have to be a church member to attend. Why don't you come along?"

On the journey home, Punam said, "You have to go."

"Well," I said. "Dave Godfrey told me that if they wanted to work with me they'd find a way."

I decided I had nothing to lose. I knew I could trust Keith Hudson.

8

Magic Circle

It was a rainy Thursday evening at the beginning of February 2004. I found myself outside the side entrance of Vestry Road Spiritualist Church. I felt very uneasy as I pushed the door open and walked down the corridor, through the main hall, and into the kitchen at the back of the church.

The air was thick with cigarette smoke. This was definitely something I would have to get used to. There were four kitchen tables, each of which was covered with a gaily-decorated plastic tablecloth. The kitchen was filled with the sounds of people enjoying each other's company. They sat around the tables and puffed away at their cigarettes, occasionally flicking ash into metal ashtrays strategically placed on each table. Keith Hudson sat with them collecting money (one pound fifty if you were working, one pound if unemployed) and making a note of attendees on a tiny writing pad.

He introduced me to everybody.

"This is Ian, the doctor I was telling you about. I've known him since he was 18."

The group consisted of informally dressed people of all ages and from all walks of life. The smoking was something else. I soon got chatting and, before I knew it, it was time to start.

There were about 20 of us. We sat on chairs arranged in a circle in the church hall. Keith explained the proceedings.

"I'll say an opening prayer and then we'll all open up. For those who haven't done this before, just breathe deeply from the stomach, not the chest. We're going to use our inner eye," he pointed to his forehead, "not the physical eyes. Imagine that with each breath you're drawing light up from your feet, up your legs, along your spine to your neck, and then up to the top of your head. Once you've done that, then you're open. Relax, keep your hands on your lap, and don't cross your arms or your legs."

I tried to loosen up, obviously unsuccessfully.

Sitting next to me was Jeff, a short, cadaverously thin man in his late thirties. He wore a pair of glasses with battered frames, which seemed slightly too large for his face. His head was shaved and elaborate tattoos decorated his bare forearms.

Jeff leaned close and whispered, "For God's sake, Doc. Just relax. Nothing's gonna happen to you."

I wasn't sure about that. I wasn't sure whether I wanted anything to happen or not. You didn't need to be psychic to sense my unease.

We began with Keith taking us through a short, guided meditation. We were to imagine walking through a beautiful garden. On our walk we would meet various individuals. At the end of the meditation, he asked each of us if we'd seen anything and, if so, to describe what we'd experienced. It was very relaxing.

After the guided meditation, Keith explained that, on instruction from his spirit guide, he'd allocated everyone a number. This could be any number from one up to the total number of attendees. He'd only tell us what our numbers were at the end of the clairvoyance session.

In the meantime, we were to relax and ask to be given messages from the spirit world that would have some meaning for any of our fellow circle members. We should wait for messages in the form of thoughts or images to occur to us. We then had to call our messages out to Keith, who would make a note of them.

Having received a message, Keith told us we shouldn't expect to know directly who it was for. Apparently, his spirit guide had made arrangements with our spirit guides that we would be given the number the recipient had been allocated by Keith, rather than the recipient's name. At that point, we couldn't know which number belonged to which person; we'd only find this out from Keith once all the messages had been given.

"Contemplate, don't concentrate," was his advice.

If any of us thought we'd received a message, we were to guess the number of the person we thought it was intended for. Then we had to tell Keith.

At the end of the clairvoyance session, Keith would collate the messages and numbers we'd given him with the numbers he'd assigned to the circle members. This enabled him to know which message was for which person.

Keith would then go to each member of the circle in turn and read out any messages they'd been given. We would discuss these as a group, exploring what each message might mean.

This had the advantage of discounting any pre-existing knowledge we might have regarding any individual. Clearly, we wouldn't know until the end which message was for which person. Keith claimed our spirit guides would know and would make sure the right person got the right message.

Despite these elaborate precautions, it was all very laid-back and a bit vague.

After a silence, someone said, "Keith, I see a bunch of roses."

"All right. Who's it for?"

"I can't see a number."

"Then go and ask them." "Them" meaning the appropriate spirit guide.

Someone saw a volcano spewing out lava for number five. Keith thought for a moment and asked what color the lava was.

"Red," was the answer.

"Red's for energy. Maybe that person needs energy."

Hmm, I thought, or maybe they were going to blow their top. Someone else saw a cat with kittens for number 14. And so on. This was nothing like I expected. It seemed to be a jumble of images, some symbolic, some possibly relating to something that had happened or was going to happen.

I decided to just go with it. So I thought of something. What came to mind was a whirlwind. In my mind's eye, the whirlwind shrank and entered a small cup. I wondered what it meant. Then I laughed to myself. It was obvious, really. Now what number could it be for? I tried to think of a number. How could I choose? I didn't have the faintest idea. I guessed 11.

"I've got something, Keith," I said.

"Good. What is it?"

"Storm in a teacup for number 11." I felt relieved that I had something to say.

"Well done. We'll see what that's about later."

At the end, Keith told us how he'd allocated the numbers.

He said his spirit guide had told him who to make number 1, and then told him to go clockwise around the circle from there.

Number 11 turned out to be Rod, a gray-haired, rather thickset truck-driver. Several others had given him messages that evening as well.

When I told him what I'd seen he shrugged his shoulders and said, "There's been a bit of an argument at home. It'll blow over. So thanks for that."

Rod's partner was a devout Christian, and she didn't approve of his interest in psychic matters.

Eventually it was time to finish. Keith closed the circle with a simple prayer of thanks. We all retired to the kitchen, which became full of cigarette smoke once again. It looked as if an hour without tobacco was just too much for most of them.

"I'm not sure I'm any good at this, Keith," I said.

"Oh, I don't know," said Keith. "You got something. You followed the meditation."

"Yes, I could follow the meditation all right. I've got a good imagination. My message was a bit crappy, though."

Keith made a sound that was a cross between a snort and a laugh. "You'd be surprised how many people get nothing."

The next day after my morning clinic, I was telling some of the receptionists about my experiences at the psychic development circle.

"So, what was it like?" asked Carol.

"To be honest, it's nothing amazing. We all just sat in a circle and tried to focus on the first image that came into our heads. It's the complete opposite of what they teach you at medical school."

"Does anybody get any messages from spirits?" asked Marie. "I'm not sure I'd like that."

I thought about this for a moment, then said, "Well, as far as they're concerned, you're asking your spirit guides for messages which come in the form of images or thoughts. The important thing is that you just have to accept these things uncritically, give them out and then try to work out if they have any significance. How you differentiate them from your own thoughts...well, that's another question. Maybe we were just deluding ourselves. I really don't know."

"So, do you think you'll go again?" asked Carol.

"Oh, yes. I think I'll just go along with it and see what happens. At least it's something different. I've got nothing to lose except my mind, and I lost that years ago."

"Yes," agreed Carol, reaching to answer the phone. "You'd have to be crazy to work here."

9

Contact

I soon got used to the weekly psychic development circle and began to look forward to it. We met every Thursday evening. The circle began at 8 p.m. and lasted exactly one hour. People started coming into the church from 7 p.m. for a chat and a smoke. I had to get used to reeking of cigarette smoke when I got home. It was worth it, though; the circle was a complete antidote to my usual working day.

As a doctor, you're trained to analyze every situation in a logical manner. You have to weigh up various diagnostic and therapeutic options. Over time, you do this automatically. With experience and knowledge of your patients, you begin to develop an instinct. Eventually, you learn to trust your gut feeling. Experienced doctors talk about this gut feeling, and everyone in medicine knows it's important. Yet there's no formal training in this. It's just something that develops. But at the psychic development circle, and with a group of strangers, most of whom were not particularly educated to any great degree, I was learning how to tap into this instinct.

My education and training hindered me. I was so used to analyzing my thoughts that I would question everything. I had to learn how to put my logical mind to one side. I could then just focus on thoughts and images as they would appear to me. It was important not to discount these—quite the reverse. Instead of ignoring the first faint ideas that came into my mind, I had to be prepared to encourage them and then present them to Keith. Analysis would be useful and important, but later on, and definitely not in the formal, logical way I was used to. Instead, we conducted the analysis of the thoughts and images presented by the members of the circle in a more symbolic manner. For example, if you thought of a red flower for someone, perhaps it meant the person needed energy, red being the symbolic color of physical energy in esoteric tradition.

It would have been easy for me to dismiss all this. However, I was impressed by the abilities of some of the more advanced members of the group.

Maureen approached me one evening after we'd closed the circle down and were clearing the chairs away. She was a gentle and rather nervous woman in her mid-sixties who was training as a healer.

"Who was the man in German uniform I saw behind you?" she asked.

"German uniform? I haven't got a clue. What sort of uniform?"

"I think it was Second World War uniform. Could he be anyone in your family?"

"Maureen, I don't think it's likely I've ever had any German Second World War officers in my family. What did he look like?"

"He was quite young, in his twenties. I think he used to drive a tank. He was tall, thin, fair and quite impatient. He was standing behind you tapping his foot like he was trying to get through to you. Do you know any German people?"

I shrugged my shoulders. My elderly relative Lotti had been born in Germany. The Nazis had killed her family in the concentration camps. She'd come to England aged 17 as a refugee on the final kindertransport and eventually married my cousin Willy. I thought it unlikely that she'd have a dead German officer from the Second World War attached to her.

The only other person I knew with German connections was my patient Elli. I'd known Elli for 20 years. She was a tall and imposing woman who'd grown up in Germany during the war and lived through the bombing of Hamburg. After the war, she'd married Tony, an English soldier in the British occupying forces, who'd brought her to England.

I'd looked after Tony when he was dying of cancer 12 years before. Lately, Elli had developed respiratory problems and I often needed to visit her at home. I'd come to know her and her daughter Sue very well. Possibly this officer was linked to Elli.

"There's only one person I can think of. Maybe he belongs to her?"

"Well, he told me he'd let you know."

I wondered how he was going to do that.

On my way home from the circle I considered calling in on Elli but immediately dismissed the idea. It wasn't hard to imagine how she might feel about her physician dropping in on her at half past nine on a winter's evening to ask her about deceased Second World War German officers. But it would at least have been nice to know his name.

The next day, as I logged onto the clinic's computer system and reviewed the morning's appointments, I noticed Elli had booked to see me.

That's strange, I thought. There I was, considering visiting her to ask her about this dead soldier, and she turns up in my waiting room. I wondered how to broach the subject. As I instructed the computer to call Elli, I wished Maureen had told me the soldier's name.

KARLHEINZ.

Now, where did that come from? I hadn't heard it. On the other hand, perhaps I *had* heard it, but with a sort of inner ear, rather like you would imagine an object with the mind's eye. I suppose you could call it the "mind's ear." Yet there was an almost physical sensation of location associated with it. It was as if I'd sort of "felt" the name, at the back of my head. It was hard to judge.

This put me in a quandary. I was aching to ask Elli if she knew this man but I couldn't imagine how I might broach the subject without her thinking I was bonkers.

Elli had come for a repeat prescription. After I'd given it to her, I mentioned I'd met a medium the evening before.

"I don't know if you believe in that sort of thing..." I said, tentatively.

Elli's eyes brightened. She seemed pleased to talk about such matters.

"Oh, yes. I've always believed. Ever since Tony died. My neighbor at number 21, Maisie, she's a clairvoyant. She's very good and I often talk to her about things."

"Ah," I said, feeling on more solid ground. "Yes. Well, that's good. The reason I mentioned this is because this medium described a young man in German Second World War uniform. She thought he was a tank driver. As you're the only person from Germany I know, I wondered if it meant anything to you."

I described the tall, impatient, fair-haired soldier Maureen had seen behind me. I wish I'd told her the name that had popped into my head, but I didn't, mainly because I thought it was just my imagination.

"That sounds like Karlheinz," she said.

My voice jumped a few octaves higher. "Really?"

"Karlheinz. Yes. He was my boyfriend. I was 18 years old and he was 19. He was in a Panzer division. You've described him quite well, especially tapping his foot like that. I never heard from him after he got sent to the Eastern Front. I've always wondered if he survived the war. You see, after I met Tony and we came to England, it was impossible to find out anything—so many men had been killed. I think I always knew something bad had happened to him."

I was very surprised at this. What surprised me most was the name. Because Maureen hadn't told me the German soldier's name, I'd assumed my intuition was just imagination. Maybe it wasn't. I tried to recall the feeling I'd had when I'd "imagined" the soldier's name. Looking back, it would have been so easy to dismiss it as one of my own thoughts. There was certainly a difference, but it was hard to define and very easy to miss.

Elli left my room as pleased as Punch. There was no doubt about it; Maureen's message had struck a chord. And it was strange how she'd given it to me the evening before Elli was booked to see me. On the other hand, though, I wondered if I'd just made a lucky guess with the name.

A few weeks later something similar happened. Again, it was from Maureen. We were sitting in circle one evening, and this time she gave me her message indirectly, using Keith's number technique. The message seemed a bit vague and really didn't mean much to me. It was simply this: "I can see a bunch of lilies."

I wrote it down in my notebook and thought no more of it.

At the time, my in-laws were looking to move down to London. They were considering buying a bungalow. They'd just viewed one and needed to hire a surveyor. Two days after I'd received the message about the bunch of lilies, I was exercising in the gym. As luck or fate would have it, I met one of my patients named Lily whom I knew very well. We started chatting and she mentioned she was leaving Enfield.

"Where are you moving to?" I asked.

"We're moving to a little village in Essex not far from Stansted Airport. Stansted Mountfichet."

I knew of the place. The headquarters of the Spiritualists' National Union was at Stansted Hall, which was just outside Stansted Mountfichet. I told her my in-laws were looking for a good surveyor.

"I'll give you the details of our surveyor. He's extremely good and not too expensive," she said.

I was getting dressed after my workout when I made the connection with Maureen's message. It must have been Lily saying she was moving to Stansted Mountfichet, with its Spiritualist connections, that jogged my memory. I wondered if I was getting a nudge from someone or something to take note of what Lily had told me. Perhaps the lilies weren't flowers but people. I recalled that Maureen had mentioned a bunch of lilies, which obviously meant more than one. I thought about all the Lilies I'd come across. The only other Lily I knew was another one of my patients. When I thought about it, I realized this too was significant. This other Lily was a well-known local real estate agent. I made a mental note to phone her the next day when I was back in the clinic.

When I looked at my appointments the next morning, I was surprised to find that Lily the real estate agent had made an appointment to see me for 8:30 that morning. She was waiting for me to call her into my office.

I had to tell her my story. Lily was very interested in what I had to say and mentioned she was very receptive to this kind of thing. She often had hunches and intuitions herself and was quite pleased to have been part of a message given by a psychic. She thought the bungalow was probably overpriced.

That night, I dreamed I was driving home. But on my way, I decided to visit a couple of friends, Mike and Louise, who lived in a large house nearby. In my dream, I turned into Mike and Louise's driveway. But instead of their house, there was a huge, old mansion. The mansion was full of painters and decorators who were fixing up the place. I noticed that instead of being in Enfield as it is now, I seemed to be in Enfield as it used to be, many years in the past. Rather than rows of houses,

I could see, from the vantage of a sweeping front yard, vistas of sunny hillsides. Of course, this being a dream, I wasn't in the least bit surprised. I was, however, surprised to see a car standing in the driveway. I know very little about cars and care even less about them. However, I knew the car was a royal-blue convertible Saab Turbo 900.

When I woke up the next day, the image of the house and front yard, and especially the blue car, remained very vivid in my mind.

In clinic the next day, I noticed that Lily's son, Christopher, had booked in to see me. I'd never met him before.

"Thought I'd come for some advice. Mum saw you yesterday and she suggested I make an appointment."

We discussed his medical concerns and I was easily able to reassure him. I asked him about his job. I'd assumed he worked at his mother's real estate agency but he didn't.

"No. I work for Saab in their new showroom in the High Street," he explained.

By now I was beginning to see how these things worked. Someone was trying to tell me something.

"Really?" I said. "I had no idea. Tell me, Chris, do they give you a company car?"

"Yes," he said.

"Would that be a royal-blue convertible Saab Turbo 900?"

"How on earth did you know that?"

"Actually, I dreamed about it last night."

He gave me a peculiar look.

"Mum said you were a bit psychic, like her." He stood up to leave. "I bet that's useful in your job."

It had been a strange sequence of events. One coincidence had led to another, which in turn had led to more. It challenged my ability to explain it away scientifically. Hard as I might try, I just could not believe it was merely random. Naturally, I

65

told my new acquaintances at the development circle. They listened politely but took it in stride.

"That's how it works," said Keith, simply. "By the way, you mentioned Stansted Hall. Have you ever been there?"

"No," I said. "I've heard about the place, though. A few years ago, I had a patient who I treated with hypnosis. She was training to be a healer at Stansted Hall. She told me all about it. I hear it's a nice place."

"It's really lovely," agreed Keith. "It was owned by Arthur Findlay. He was a stockbroker who became a Spiritualist, and when he died he donated his house to the movement. It's now called the Arthur Findlay College and it's a fantastic place. The gardens are beautiful. You should go one day during one of their open weeks."

"Maybe I will. When's the next one?"

"Funny you should mention that. Next week, in fact."

Keith showed me the prospectus. There were different events all week. My eye was drawn to the following Saturday. There was a one-day course in mediumship for beginners. No need to book, just turn up. It was very reasonably priced at 10 pounds for the whole day.

"I think I'll go," I said. "Maybe I'm meant to go. Perhaps that was what the message about the bunch of lilies was trying to tell me. It's like a puzzle. Maybe they wanted to see if I could figure it out."

Jeff expertly flicked some ash from his cigarette. He nodded sagely, looked at Keith, and said, "I think he's getting the hang of this, don't you?"

10

Spooks' Hall

It's an easy 45-minute drive from Enfield to the headquarters of the Spiritualists' National Union. Turn off the M11 and follow the signs to the Stansted Airport long-term parking lot. Go past the parking lot and proceed for about a mile. Cross over the M11 and then turn sharp right into the grounds of Stansted Hall. The locals call it "Spooks' Hall."

Stansted Hall is everything the headquarters of a Spiritualist organization should be. In the style of an Edwardian country house, with gardens to match, you wouldn't be surprised if you were greeted by Jeeves and Wooster, followed by a retinue of headless ghosts, white ladies, and spectral hounds.

The decor is dark and heavy with oak paneling, paintings, and brass and wooden light fixtures. You would almost expect the eyes of the portraits to move. They don't, but Arthur Findlay, who donated this grand old house, is there in all his glory, his portrait hanging above the reception desk in the entrance hall.

I was in luck that Saturday—there were three empty places for the mediumship study day. I booked myself a place on the course and decided to let go of my scientific preconceptions and just relax into the day. Our teacher was Paul and, apart from him, I was the only male in the group of 20. We were in a large, plushly carpeted room with upright chairs arranged in a circle.

First off, Paul had each of us stand up in front of the rest of the group. He wanted to see what we could pick up from each other. When it was my turn, I focused on the woman sitting directly opposite me. All I could see in my mind was what seemed like green garden netting. I could see a man's face behind the netting. It didn't mean much to me and I couldn't get anything else. I felt a bit embarrassed and sat down. Paul clearly wasn't impressed with that.

As I sat down, I felt myself drawn towards a woman to my right. It felt like a tugging sensation somewhere in my head. As I became aware of this, I experienced a series of images, which flashed into my mind very quickly. I could see the woman standing in a very white room, which was filled with large stainless steel equipment. She was wearing white overalls and a white pork-pie hat and was putting on a pair of yellow rubber gloves. I felt she was in a dairy. I made a mental note to ask her about this. Then Paul split us up into pairs.

My partner was a very young-looking and slightly bewildered woman named Nicky. She'd told the group she'd recently started seeing balls of light flashing around her bedroom at night. Paul had said he was very interested in her story because this was how he'd become aware of his own mediumistic abilities.

The aim of our initial exercise was to work at what Paul called the psychic level. He was very specific about what he meant by this: all mediums are psychic, but not all psychics are mediums. He explained that the process was like a radio working at different frequencies. At the lower frequencies you can pick up information about people and objects around you. This is what he called the psychic level. However, if you focus on someone and then try to tune into the higher frequencies, you can then pick up any spirits connected to that person who may be trying to communicate. He called this the spiritual or higher level.

As we were initially going to work at the psychic level, the object of this first exercise was to see what we could pick up about our partners. Nicky and I sat opposite each other. I took the first turn. I tried to still my mind and go with whatever first impressions came to me. Very gradually, I began to feel that she worked with people in a counseling role and that she'd recently been given a job with more responsibility. Apparently, I was spot on. She was a clinical psychologist, newly appointed as head of her department. I was pleasantly surprised at this.

Nicky said she saw me in a clinical setting, examining people's backs. I asked her to guess what I did and she said she thought I was possibly an osteopath. As I was a physician with an interest in back disorders, I thought she was very accurate.

For the next exercise we switched partners. My new partner was the woman whom I'd visualized as being in a dairy. Her name was Linda.

Again, we had to sit opposite each other. This time, however, we had to try and "go higher" and tune into a more spiritual level.

I told her I'd imagined her in a dairy, earlier on in the group exercise.

"That's because I've just finished a five-day cheese making course," she said.

"You're kidding me!"

"No. You saw me in the room where they curdle the milk. See what else you can pick up."

"Okay."

I closed my eyes and tried to clear my mind. After a few seconds, I became aware of an image of a small mahogany table. It had a lacy tablecloth draped over it. Precisely placed on the tablecloth were lots of little glass ornaments. I also became aware of someone standing next to me. I opened my eyes. It was Paul, observing how we were doing.

I told Linda what I'd seen.

"That's my collection table at home. I collect glass," she said.

I felt very pleased with myself.

Paul, however, shook his head and said, "That's just psychic stuff. Anyone can do that. Go up a level."

Never mind. Even if Paul wasn't impressed with me, I most certainly was. It was as if I'd managed to plug my mind into someone else's. I felt curiously elated but it was beginning to take its toll. I could feel a headache coming on. I ignored it and tried to "go up a level."

"How do I go up?" I asked.

"Imagine you've got porcupine quills running down your spine," said Paul. "Visualize them sticking out like little aerials that can tune into spirit. Then ask for an object."

"How do you mean 'an object'?" I asked.

"Ask them to give you an object which has some meaning for Linda. It could be a car, a plate, or a ring—something like that. Describe it and see if it means anything to her."

Okay, I'd give it a go. I tried to visualize my quills bristling behind me.

I saw what looked like a hand bell. That turned into a half-formed image in my mind. It was hard to describe. It looked like two wooden paddles or short oars but they were somehow joined together. As I described what I was seeing, I was gesturing with my hands, waving them in and out rhythmically. Linda couldn't understand what I was talking about.

Paul walked off shaking his head, totally unimpressed.

"Linda," I said, "I get the impression these paddles belonged to an elderly lady. I think she was your aunt."

"Well, the only aunt I have in spirit is my Aunt Nora. I don't know what the paddles are about. Now, if you'd said bellows then I would have understood. She used to have a pair of old-fashioned bellows by her fire for show and I always used to play with them when I was a kid."

As Linda said this, she looked at my hands. I was moving them as if working a pair of bellows. She smiled, raised her eyebrows, and mimicked what I was doing with my hands.

"Good Lord!" I said, as I realized what my hand movements might signify.

I didn't say it, but it occurred to me that if I'd said "bell" and "oars" I'd have been close to the word "bellows." That's pushing it a bit, I thought.

"Oh. Yes, of course. A pair of paddles joined together with something," said Linda. "I think you got my Aunt Nora. That's great!"

I looked around for Paul, but he'd gone.

Linda tried to pick up something from me and described a tall, smartly-dressed man wearing a dark suit and tie. I couldn't place him.

It was now lunchtime. I felt extremely tired and I'd developed a splitting headache. Luckily, I had some painkillers in my car.

Lunch was roast beef and Yorkshire pudding, inexpensive and well-cooked. The dining hall was packed and I was last in the queue. I was carrying a full dinner plate looking up and down the long refectory tables for a vacant seat. A dark-haired, dark-eyed woman in her early middle years caught my eye and smiled. She was sitting at a table with two younger men, a slightly older woman and two elderly ladies. There was an empty space at the table. I sat down opposite her and said hello. Her name was Jan and she was teaching the course on aura photographs and color therapy. The two men were attending her course and she seemed to know them quite well. The other three women had flown down from Newcastle for the weekend.

Before I could say anything about myself, Jan said something rather peculiar. "You're a bit of a martial artist."

This took me aback. I'd learned karate up to brown belt level. But that had been many years before. I'd long since given it up. I wondered how this related to anything.

She then elaborated: "With energy. You're a bit of a martial artist with energy. You know what I mean." I was sure I didn't.

"No. I don't," I said.

"When you're with your patients."

I was quite certain I hadn't told her I was a doctor.

"You're always giving out and receiving energy, deflecting it, converting it. You're a real expert."

"Oh," I said. "Thanks." I wasn't certain what else to say. It was quite the oddest conversation I'd ever had with a stranger.

"Only," she continued, "you need to keep your explanations a bit simpler for your patients. Make sure you speak at their level. So they can understand you."

Then the penny dropped. I remembered the dream I'd had, about giving out all that "blue."

"Are you talking about healing?" I asked.

"Yes, I am. And other things too. It's all about energy, you know. We all give out and receive subtle energy. I can tell you're really good at it. Why don't you come to my color therapy course one day?"

"Look, how do you know all this about me? How did you know I'm a doctor?"

"I can see auras," she explained. "I've always been able to see them. It's how peoples' energy appears to me. Some people can see it, you know. Others feel it."

Eventually, Jan left with the two men and I sat alone with the ladies from Newcastle. They had a small home circle where they developed their psychic awareness. Once every couple of years they flew down for the open weekend at Stansted Hall. It was very convenient for them with Stansted Airport being so near. We had a pleasant conversation. One of the ladies used to be a nurse and had some fascinating stories to tell about nursing dying patients. She'd witnessed all sorts of things that had made her interested in Spiritualism.

"I can't count the number of times my patients described relatives who'd passed over and come to visit them just before it was their own turn to pass." Then she became wistful. "I expect when it's my turn my husband will come and get me."

It was two o'clock and by now the dining room was almost empty. I still had the remnants of my headache and wondered whether I ought to call it a day. Thankfully, I didn't. Instead, I decided to see what Paul had planned for the afternoon.

To start with, Paul explained that spirit communication could be densely packed with information. Any images received could well have several layers of meaning. He illustrated this by picking out a woman from the group and writing on a whiteboard any images that came into his mind. These were images of a father and son, a submarine, a sea-chart, and a telescope.

Paul asked her if she could relate to these. She told him that her father and grandfather had both served in the Royal Navy on submarines during the Second World War. In fact, her father had been on the first submarine to sink a German U-boat.

He then used the same images to describe what was happening in her life. She was currently "all at sea" and had recently been looking for a new direction in her life (the map). She now had the ability to see where she was heading (the telescope). She nodded avidly, clearly relating to the message. He then asked if this set of images meant anything to any of the other members of the group, but no one could think of a decent connection. He finished by making the following point:

"The spirit world has some very clever people in it. They have developed very powerful techniques to aid communication through what is often a very difficult connection. Never make the mistake of thinking it's all down to us on this side. It depends on both sides."

We paired up again. This time I sat opposite Hayley, a fair-haired woman in her twenties. Once again, we had to see what we could pick up. Hayley tuned in to me first. She picked up a smartly-dressed man in a suit. It was the same description Linda had given to me. I really couldn't place this man. Hayley was pleased to know that, whoever he was, she'd confirmed Linda's impressions.

It was now my turn. Again, Paul was observing.

I focused on Hayley and thought I could see a thinner, older woman standing behind her. To my mind, she looked like Jane from the Walthamstow circle. I wondered what on earth Jane would be doing there. I described her to Hayley.

"That's my mum," she said.

No, it isn't, I thought, I was thinking of Jane.

"Is she in spirit?" asked Paul.

"No," said Hayley.

"Okay," said Paul. "You've got a psychic link. Anyone can do that. Now try and go up."

That annoyed me. No, Paul, on my planet not everyone can do that. Besides, I had a clear image of Jane. I thought I'd challenge him.

"Paul, I'm not describing Hayley's mum, I can see someone else. It's someone I know named Jane."

Let's see how you get out of that one, then.

However, Paul had an answer.

"Yes," he said, "but you've never met Hayley's mum, have you?"

That was true.

He explained what he meant: "What they do is use the images already in your mind. They find the one Hayley will be able to understand. You may be describing Jane but she'll take it to be her mum. Go on. Now you've got the link, go higher."

I tried to relax and imagine I had porcupine quills extending out from my spine between my shoulder blades.

In my mind's eye, I could still clearly see Jane, standing behind Hayley. But behind her I became aware of an altogether more shadowy presence. This was a woman, older than Jane, with gray hair and wearing a floral dress. She was smiling and had her hands on Jane's shoulders. Then the image changed and became more vivid. I experienced the startlingly clear vision of a crystal chandelier, which took up my entire inner field of view. It radiated a powerful light and I could clearly see rainbow colors refracted from the cut crystal.

With that, I felt I'd suddenly been handed a vast amount of information about this woman: as if she'd somehow dropped it into my head, all at once.

I heard myself saying, very quickly, "I can see a crystal chandelier. There wasn't just one—she had lots of them. Her house was full of crystal chandeliers. She was very proud of her house. It was always neat. She was very close to you. I think she was your grandmother or maybe your grandmother's sister. She had a stroke and was incapacitated towards the end of her life. She was very ill but she really didn't want to die. She's happy now and she's really pleased to have got through to you."

Then I started to splutter. I felt an intense happiness welling up in my chest. It became impossible to contain it and I burst into tears. Everyone in the room was looking at me. I couldn't help it. I was overcome with emotion. Then I lost the connection. It just went. I could remember what I'd seen but the vividness of the information was no longer so apparent. The emotions I'd been feeling had suddenly disappeared, as if someone had thrown a switch. However, the image of the crystal chandelier remained very clear—I can still recall it.

Hayley was looking at me intensely.

"That was my aunt. My great aunt. You got her exactly right. And she loved crystal chandeliers. But the best bit is the fact that you're crying."

"Why?" I asked. I felt extremely foolish. I hadn't cried in public since I was a child.

"Because nine years or so before she died she'd had a stroke, like you said. It affected her brain. She became much more emotional. She used to cry whenever she was happy."

I was pleased but I felt as if I'd been put through the wringer. My headache was back and I was completely drained of energy.

Paul didn't say much then but afterwards he came up to me and said, "You have to be a bit more careful. You should never say, 'She didn't want to die'; that's not very comforting for the relatives. It's not very professional. And also, you've got to learn not to be affected so much by the conditions you encounter."

I could take his point about being more professional. I wasn't sure I understood what he meant by the term "conditions."

Paul sensed my confusion. "You'll experience lots of different emotions from the spirit people you contact. You have to learn how to be aware of them but not let them affect you. You've got a lot of work to do."

It had been one hell of a day. My expectations combined with the ambiance of the place seemed to have had a beneficial effect. I'd had absolutely no trouble receiving images and thoughts, and they'd been remarkably accurate. But I felt completely done in and found the drive back to Enfield difficult because I was tired. This tiredness persisted for the next week. I dragged myself to work and yawned my way through my clinics.

I discussed my experiences at the psychic development

circle. Everyone agreed that the biggest problem when doing this sort of work was exhaustion.

"It can be very draining," said Keith. "I only open up when I'm working. When you've finished, you must make sure you shut down again properly. That's something you've got to learn to do. Don't worry, you'll get there. Just give yourself time."

11

Opening Up

I continued to attend the psychic development circle at Vestry Road Spiritualist Church every Thursday evening. I've already explained how we would give blind readings. By blind, I mean we didn't give messages directly to a specific person but to a number representing the recipient. Keith Hudson was the only one who knew which number belonged to any particular individual and he wouldn't tell us until he'd collated all the messages at the end of the evening.

Most development circles don't use this technique, and many psychics and mediums would find it a little peculiar. Nevertheless, with my more scientific background, I found it made the whole process much more believable. It's true we could have been getting unconscious clues from Keith, but at least he'd made an effort to limit other possible sources of information.

I noticed some interesting patterns. For example, I went through phases of tracking the same individual from week to week, even though Keith gave each of us a different number every time we practiced. For a while I seemed to have a particular affinity with Jane and she with me. In fact, my first really impressive message was to Jane.

I'd been experimenting with different visualization techniques. My method at the time involved imagining an old-fashioned movie screen displaying those flickering numbers you used to see counting down before the movie started. I'd try to imagine the countdown stopping at a number and then an image forming on the screen. That evening the numbers stopped at nine and I got a very clear image of a well-dressed man with a mustache and slicked-back hair.

He gave me the name George and a message to "check the vacation arrangements."

I can't say I exactly heard this message. It was more a sort of internal knowing. I wrote it down. At the end of the clairvoyance session, as we were going through the messages, Keith told Jane she was number 9 that evening. I gave her my message and she nodded vigorously.

"That's definitely my Uncle George. He's come through before. I don't know what the message is about, though."

I ticked off my message in my spiral-bound notebook and placed a question mark by it—a probable hit but not sure about the message.

The next week, as we were gathering in the kitchen, Jane handed me an old photograph. "I found this and I thought you'd be interested."

It was a picture of Jane's Uncle George. He looked like the man I'd described the week before.

Jane continued: "I booked our summer vacation on the internet. I've never done that before. So anyway, I checked the arrangements, like you told me to, and it turned out they hadn't received any money so they weren't going to reserve the vacation for us."

By now everyone was listening to her story and I could feel my credibility soaring.

That was a clear example of a good message. The problem was, though, that often the images received were symbolic or metaphorical. For example, seeing a cat climbing out of a bag might mean someone had "let the cat out of the bag." Just to complicate matters, sometimes things would appear to be metaphorical when in fact they accurately described something that had happened or perhaps was going to happen.

The clearest example of this was the message I gave to Rod,

the truck driver. That evening he was number 6. Associated with that number I had a clear vision of a fish tank in a sitting room somewhere. Only...it was empty and I had a sense of loss. I described what I saw and said I thought it was symbolic and probably meant he'd lost something. Otherwise, I couldn't possibly imagine why I would be seeing an empty fish tank.

Rod leaned forward and looked at me. "Actually, Doc, it's the fish tank in my living room. It's empty because my piranhas died last week."

There was laughter at my over-earnest attempt at interpretation.

One week, Keith Hudson suggested we should try to give messages in the more traditional manner. Instead of using the number technique, we were to simply see if we felt drawn to anyone in particular.

That night there was a big circle; there must have been 25 or more in the group as some new people had turned up. The church hall was in darkness except for a candle, which had been placed on the floor in the center of the circle. Its flame cast eerie giant flickering shadows of the participants onto the walls.

I looked around the circle to see if I could pick up anything. Sitting opposite me, I noticed a young woman in her late twenties who hadn't attended before. I thought I could see a dim cone of light behind her. It appeared to start from just above her head, fading rapidly to nothing just below her shoulder level as it fanned out downwards. It's hard to explain how I saw it. It didn't appear to be merely a mental picture. But then I didn't exactly see it physically, either.

At that moment, Rod, who was seated a few chairs to her right, said, "I can see a light behind the lady over there." He pointed to the woman.

I nudged Maureen who was sitting next to me and

whispered, "I thought I saw a light or something behind her, too."

"Well, tell her what you see, don't hold onto it," urged Maureen.

Keith had been busy writing our impressions into a little notebook. Appropriately enough, he was using a Harry Potter-themed illuminated pen so he could write in the darkness.

"Keith, I've got something," I said.

"Ian. Go on."

I addressed myself to the woman. "Erm...I also thought I saw a light behind you...I'm sorry I can't remember your name."

"Joanne," she said.

"Joanne. When Rod mentioned he saw a light behind you, I also thought I saw something like a cone of light behind you."

As I started talking to her, I became aware of receiving more information.

I continued. "It seemed as if the light was like the image of a waterfall. This is very strange. As I'm talking I can see someone very much like you standing under, or behind, a waterfall."

Joanne's face lit up. "Go on. Please," she said. I grabbed for more information from...somewhere, but came up empty-handed.

I shook my head. "That's all I've got."

Keith looked over to me. "Go back and ask them for more," was all he said. He meant ask the spirits.

I sat in silence for the rest of the evening, trying to see what else I could pick up for Joanne. I approached her at the end of the session. I felt a bit stupid but told her what else I'd received.

"I think I've got a woman who died recently. She was about your age. In fact, she looks very much like you but in personality she's different. She's calmer and more levelheaded.

I get the impression you two were very close and you looked after her somehow. She lost a lot of weight before she died and you were concerned about her not eating. The waterfall is very important, which is why she showed it to me."

Joanne nodded. "Can you tell me her name?" she asked.

I laughed, nervously. "That's difficult for me. I'm really not good with names, I tend to see things rather than hear them but, at a guess, I'd go for something that sounds like Lucilla or Cilla, maybe even Celia. I'm not sure. Does this mean anything to you?"

She looked at me and smiled. "Thank you. I knew if I came here she'd get in touch with me. It's my twin sister, Cecilia. She died a couple of months ago from bowel cancer. She couldn't eat and lost a lot of weight, as you said."

"Did she look like you?" I asked.

"We were identical twins." Joanne looked sad.

"Why was she showing me a waterfall?"

"Just before Cecilia died we went to Aysgarth Falls in Yorkshire. It was one of her favorite places. I'm really pleased you contacted my sister. I know I don't have to worry about her now. Thanks."

That was the only time Joanne came to our circle. I guess she'd found what she'd been looking for.

Gradually, as the weeks passed, I got better at giving messages. I experimented with different ways of working out which number the message was for. The movie screen idea soon became boring. I changed tack. I pretended I was looking at a flip-chart and someone was drawing a picture on it. I also imagined there was a number written in the top left hand corner of the flip-chart. What I received were often humorous-looking cartoons.

For example, I had a message that turned out to be for

Jeff. I saw a cartoon character standing by some broken paving stones. The cartoon character was wearing a yellow miner's helmet so I got the impression there was a problem with some groundwork, possibly subsidence.

In fact, Jeff's patio had, just that day, fallen into a hole that had suddenly appeared in his backyard. That was impressive.

One evening, I had an image of washing machines and dishwashers leaking water. Once again, this was for Jeff.

The following week, as I came into the church, Jeff called to me across the church hall. "Hey, Doc! The next time you tell me my washing machine's going to leak, make sure you give me the name of a decent plumber."

On the whole, I was pleased with my progress. What it all meant was another matter. One thing I was sure about: I wasn't just receiving random impressions. There was a process of some sort at work. If it was just random guesswork then my accuracy should have been fairly consistent overall. However, I definitely noticed certain things could improve my accuracy. If I felt very lively and energetic, or if I was in a good and expansive mood, then I was very much more likely to give an accurate message. However, if I was feeling depressed or in a state of low energy my messages would be mediocre at best or, more usually, just plain wrong.

I'd also noticed something else. If I was feeling stressed out and tense, but not particularly depressed, my messages would often be much better. Also under conditions of stress, odd coincidences would start to happen, or perhaps I just noticed them more. I wondered why this should be.

12

My Spirit Guide Went Off to Work
in Manchester

It was an unseasonably cool Wednesday afternoon in May and time to meet my channeler. Her name was Eleanor, which sounded rather fitting: Eleanor the Channeler.

I wasn't sure about this channeling nonsense. Would I really find enlightenment in the London Borough of Ealing at the end of the District subway line? I didn't think so, but as I'd come this far, it seemed a shame not to go the extra mile. In order to convince myself, I decided to play a little game. I would pretend I was an investigative reporter who had to make a documentary on New Age beliefs. Alternatively, I could make believe I was a sociological researcher looking at contemporary spirituality. It was a sop to my rational side, which had lately become like a very large dog reluctant to go for a walk...

It takes two hours to travel from Enfield to Ealing using public transport. I spent every minute of those two hours asking myself why I was doing this.

Eleanor the Channeler's house was a 10-minute walk away from the station, not far from Ealing Common. It was an impressive red-brick, semi-detached affair. I hesitated fractionally in front of its painted wooden front door. What was I doing here? It would be so easy just to turn around and leave. I took a deep breath and rang the doorbell. I could see a vague approaching form through the door's single frosted glass pane. There was no turning back now.

The door was opened by a woman who looked to be in her late sixties. She was smartly-dressed, wearing a turtleneck lilac sweater and dark slacks. Her long gray hair was loose and she wore no makeup. Eleanor the Channeler. Let's be honest: Eleanor, *my* channeler. I must be bonkers.

"Come in, dear," she said. Her voice was somewhat deep and her accent was what my kids would have called classy, certainly classier than mine.

Eleanor ushered me through her hallway and into a small kitchen that evidently had once been an Edwardian scullery. She imperiously motioned towards one of her antique pine kitchen chairs. "Please sit down. And don't look so nervous."

"Well, I've never done this before," I protested.

She nodded gravely, contemplating my predicament. Then her expression brightened. "And you are my first doctor."

That was no surprise to me. I couldn't think of any other doctor who'd be prepared to go through this. Except possibly the "I've-got-an-alien-living-in-my-apartment" doctor—he might be up for it.

We sat at her kitchen table, drinking tea.

"Tell me why you have come," she commanded.

I told her about everything that had happened to me recently and about the strange events I'd experienced in the past. It all came out in a bit of a rush and she had to rein me back in.

"Oh dear," she said. "You're not very grounded, are you? I can see I'm going to have to teach you how to ground yourself. It is most important for you to protect yourself when you are going through an awakening."

Eleanor told me a little about herself. She had undergone her own "awakening" about 20 years before. A stressful situation at work had led her to re-evaluate her life. As a result, she had developed an interest in the New Age movement and joined a psychic development circle. Eventually she had become a trance medium, having formed a very close working relationship with a particular Native American spirit guide. That much I could follow. Then she said something that made no sense to me whatsoever.

"Anyway, he had to leave me a few years ago because he needed to work in Manchester. So I left the group and started on my own."

What on earth was she going on about? I thought she'd been talking about her spirit guide. Now she was telling me about some chap going off to work in Manchester. I was confused, but no more so than when listening to some of my patients. I'd long ago discovered that many people don't necessarily experience their lives as a logical sequence of events. So I let her talk and, ho-hum, sure enough, she actually was talking about her spirit guide. He really had left her to work in Manchester. Possibly, in this lady's universe, spirits commuted to work. Perhaps they took the ghost train.

"You really need to be more grounded," she told me. "I will teach you how to ground yourself and open up and then, more importantly, how to close down."

Like most doctors, I tend to have a scientific approach to things. It's all part of the training. This meant I really needed to understand what grounding, opening up, and closing down actually meant. Sure, at first glance it seemed obvious: if you were going to open up to any form of psychic work, you had to keep a sense of reality. However, I sensed there was a deeper, more technical explanation regarding their fuller meaning.

It was my patient Dave Godfrey who explained how he understood these terms. He'd come to see me a few days before so I could check his blood pressure.

"Ian. Think of the caduceus."

"You mean the medical symbol? The two snakes intertwined around a staff?"

"That's right." Dave took a pen out of his jacket pocket.

"Got a piece of paper, Ian?"

I slipped a blank piece of paper out of my laser printer and handed it to him. With his pen he drew a rough picture of the caduceus: a single upright staff with a pair of wings projecting from its top end and two snakes sinuously winding up the staff from bottom to top. The snakes crossed over each other several times and their heads met at the top of the staff, just below the wings.

Dave looked at his artwork for a second, glanced at me, and then indicated the drawing with his pen.

"The caduceus was supposedly the staff of the Ancient Greek god Hermes," he said. "The single unifying theme in all modern psychic work is energy. It's even crept into Spiritualist jargon replacing the term 'vibrations' or 'spirit power.' The idea goes like this: a flow of universal subtle energy regulates the whole of existence. There is only one type of energy but it has two directions of flow: from spirit to physical, and then back from physical to spirit. You can think of Man, who has both a physical and a spiritual body, as acting as a link, or conduit, between the two. In fact, you can think of all life as acting in this way. The physical form of the energy is at a lower frequency than the spirit form. As it flows from spirit to physical, its frequency is lowered. As it flows from physical to spirit, its frequency is raised."

I thought about this.

"So, living beings would be what? Transformers? Transducers?"

"Yes," agreed Dave. "In transforming this energy, living beings do work, and the work they do is what we term life."

"Okay. That makes sense to me."

"Good, because it's very important. Let's consider the symbol of the caduceus further. You have two currents of energy, symbolized by the snakes, forming a circuit. Notice how the snakes cross over each other several times." Dave tapped on his drawing with his pen to indicate the crossing points. "You can think of the points where they cross as centers of psychic energy."

"You mean chakras?"

"Yes. Chakra is a Sanskrit term which means wheel. Each chakra represents a crossing point of energy. Where they cross, the two opposing currents set up a rotating vortex of energy. So the word 'chakra' is quite descriptive. Traditionally, there are seven major chakras and these need to open up in order to do any form of psychic work. In order to do this you require a free flow of energy, which means you need a strong link to spirit and also to be well-grounded..."

"...in order to complete the circuit."

"Yes, in order to complete the circuit."

Eleanor took me upstairs to a back bedroom. It was a plain room and contained just a simple, straight-backed chair and the sort of examination couch you might find in my office. On the walls were old black-and-white photographs of Native Americans. She explained they were pictures of her spirit guides.

Eleanor sat me down on the chair and asked me to relax.

"I'll just take you though a grounding procedure, and then I'll teach you how to open up."

I felt a bit uncomfortable about all this and I thought I ought to let her know.

"Eleanor. Before we start, can I just say I might find it a bit difficult to relax. I can't honestly say I expected to find myself in this situation."

Eleanor brushed off my misgivings easily with a languid wave of her hand.

"I know dear. Surprising things happen when you start

to raise your awareness. I mean, imagine how surprised I was when I discovered that one of my spirit guides was a twelve-foot tall alien."

She said this perfectly calmly, as if it were the most natural thing in the world.

I thought, not another alien! I'm in a room with a crazy woman and she's standing between me and the door!

My fears were groundless. She spent the session teaching me how to visualize anchoring myself into the earth and then imagining energy rising up through my legs and my spine, opening up the seven chakras as it did so. She asked me to visualize the opening of the chakras as the opening of flower petals. She spent a long time doing this and an equally long time teaching me how to close down. She assured me that it was very important, and that with time I would be able to open up and close down very quickly. It was all quite relaxing and pleasant.

Then she closed her eyes and spoke in a deep voice she claimed belonged to her alien spirit guide. This was amusing because when she spoke in the voice of her alien spirit guide she spoke in the third person, but sometimes became mixed up ("I'm going to open my—I mean Eleanor's—eyes"). There was much lighting of candles and at one point she had me conversing with an imaginary snail-like life form on a planet in a different universe. Unfortunately, all I could visualize was Brian the Snail from the 1960s animated children's TV series, *The Magic Roundabout*, wearing his long scarf, his hat perched at a jaunty angle.

All Brian the Snail said to me was, "I dunno," like he used to on TV.

And if Brian the Snail didn't know, then neither did I.

On the way back home, standing awkwardly in a crush

of commuters on a crowded subway train in the rush hour, I wondered what it had all been about. The whole fiasco had cost me an afternoon in time and 35 pounds in cash. Not that I resented Eleanor's fee; she'd spent over two hours with me and genuinely believed in what she was doing. I'd found her chakra visualization method soothing and, in the context of what I'd been learning, it even made a kind of sense. She'd certainly managed to relax me. But then, just as I'd dropped my guard, she'd gone and wrong-footed me with the whole alien snail business, which seemed supremely silly. But of course, that's the nature of the Twilight Zone; it always keeps you guessing.

The following Thursday, I sat in the cigarette smoke-filled kitchen at Vestry Road Spiritualist Church entertaining everyone with the tale of what had happened to me at Ealing.

Keith laughed. "There's a load of people like that in this field. It attracts 'em. You've got to sort the wheat from the chaff."

I explained how she'd taught me to open up and close down.

"So," said Jeff. He took a long drag from his cigarette. "She can't have been that stupid, then."

"That's right." Keith looked serious now. "It's very important when you're doing this work to keep yourself firmly anchored to the earth. I always say that when your head's in the clouds you need your feet firmly on the ground. Think of a tree: in order for its branches to go high into the air it needs roots going down just as deep into the earth. You need to be firmly anchored; otherwise you'll be mentally swept away. And that does happen to some people."

Jeff took his cigarette out of his mouth and disdainfully puffed some smoke into the air. "Yeah. They become fuckin' space cadets."

13

The Quiet Mind

My daily round of clinics, house calls, and sorting out people's problems continued. However, I found my new interest was forcing me to think about things I'd never really considered before. I began to read books about after-death communication. I read voraciously, anything from the rigorous to the woolly-minded. I wanted to explore the mindset of people who believed in spirits, nature spirits, spirit guides, and angels. How could people hold such crazy beliefs that were so alien to my education?

At the same time, there were lots of shows to watch on TV featuring famous mediums. I found myself watching TV channels I'd never have considered viewing in the past. To my surprise, I started taking a technical interest in the proceedings.

As regards TV mediums, the view of the more experienced members of the development circle was that, while not necessarily fake, you only saw the good stuff.

June's opinion was typical. "No one can be that accurate and consistent all the time. They film a lot longer than the half-hour they show you. There are loads of messages that aren't taken that you never get to see. It's not as easy as they make it seem."

When I was in circle, I tried to silence my mind's unending chatter and just let images come as they pleased. The secret was to allow them to form, and then examine them gently when they were there, instead of dismissing them.

I began to realize there are two classes of phenomena in life: shy things and bold things. Bold things require energy and effort to grab them. They respond well to the expenditure of energy. Western society dedicates itself to bold things: bold enterprises; going for it; grabbing it while you can. On the other hand, shy things only come to you when they are ready to. Imagine waiting for a shy animal. If you run towards it, it runs away from you. The more energy you expend, the less you achieve. However if you hold out your hand and just wait, it may come to you.

This psychic stuff was a shy thing, not a bold enterprise. I had to still myself so that it came to me. This was a novel concept for me as I'd always expended a vast amount of energy pursuing my objectives. I had to learn to stop behaving like a bull in a china shop. I was thinking about this one evening, and I decided what I really needed was a quiet mind.

The next day Lynda came to see me. I'd known Lynda since I'd worked at the medical center. She was a Spiritualist and had been following my progress with interest. She was also in a development circle at a different church. Lynda was training to be a healer and a medium. Her particular gift was clairaudience. She didn't see with her mind's eye but claimed to hear very clearly with a sort of psychic inner ear. We'd had some very interesting conversations about her experiences recently.

As usual, she came to me so I could check her blood pressure prior to giving her a prescription. She took the prescription and put it in her handbag. Then she took a small book out of her handbag and handed it to me.

"Is this for me?"

"Yes," she said. "They told me to give it to you when I was meditating last night."

I looked at the cover. The book was *The Quiet Mind* by White Eagle.

"That really is amazing!" I exclaimed.

I found it hard to believe that, just the evening before, I'd decided I needed a quiet mind, and now here was one of my patients giving me a book with that title.

"Isn't it funny how they work?" said Lynda. "You'll get used to it. There's no such thing as coincidence you know."

That evening I settled down to read the book. Some research on the internet had told me that White Eagle was supposed to be a highly advanced spirit guide who'd been channeled by a medium named Grace Cook in the 1930s. Full of spiritual advice written in quite a flowery style, it was an easy read. Its rather religious perspective rankled with my secular outlook but I had to agree with the sentiments expressed: we were to be of service to others whenever possible. It certainly fit in with my medical training.

It was now June, and I'd been attending the psychic development circle for about four months. I was beginning to get a feeling for how to become aware of information I may have gained psychically. However, unlike the more experienced members of the group, I didn't sense this information being given to me by a spirit guide. In fact, I hadn't even met my spirit guide. I'd always thought I had a "higher self," but I'd merely assumed it was just a somewhat more detached part of my own mind. A few people had said they sensed a clerical man around me who was my guide but nothing more specific than that.

I had a lot of problems with the concept of spirit guides. Surely, if there happened to be any substance to paranormal phenomena, spirit guides were just a convenient fiction. Perhaps they were just a way of distancing the rational conscious mind from the irrational unconscious mind. Maybe the unconscious mind could then work unfettered from any preconceptions about what was and was not possible. But gradually I began to receive the impression that someone was trying to get my attention when I wasn't in the development circle. This was usually in the form of extremely unlikely coincidences.

For example, one day I noticed I was thinking of the name "Sutton." I recalled working with a Dr. Sutton when I was a resident at the local hospital. His daughter, Debbie, had been one of my sister's school friends. I hadn't thought about Dr. Sutton for years. He'd died unexpectedly of a heart attack when he was about 50 years old. This was some 25 years or so before, so why I should have been thinking of him was a mystery to me.

Then I began to notice the name "Sutton" everywhere: it came up in a book I was reading; I opened a map of London and my eye was drawn to Sutton in London, that sort of thing. I even mentioned to Punam the curious fact that I kept on coming across the name "Sutton" and how my friends in the psychic development circle would think it was significant.

One pleasant afternoon I thought it would make a change to go out for a drive in the countryside. My car's windshield was dirty, and the windshield washer container under the hood needed filling up. I couldn't find the windshield washer liquid anywhere and spent some considerable time looking for it all over the house and in the backyard shed. I was certain I had a bottle somewhere. In the end I gave up and filled the container with water but left space for the windshield washer liquid.

Punam and I headed off in the car to a nearby countryside park. But on the way I had an urge to go instead to the Hatfield Galleria, a large shopping mall where there was a decent bookshop. I wondered if there would be any books there about mediumship.

The Galleria parking area was almost full. There were no spaces outside so we entered the multi-level parking garage. We drove round and round, ascending level after level, until finally I spotted a space. As I headed towards this space, another car shot into it ahead of me. In frustration, I turned right and noticed there was another empty space nearby. At last! I parked the car and we got out.

I couldn't believe my eyes. On the parking lot floor in front of the car was an opened, but almost full, bottle of windshield washer liquid. We were both open-mouthed with astonishment. It was as if it had been placed there like some sort of offering. The lid was perched on top of the bottle but, as I picked it up, it became apparent why the bottle had been left there. There was no screw-thread on the lid. Its seal must have been holding it on. Whoever had bought it had undone the bottle, filled up their car's windshield washer container, and then realized the lid wouldn't stay on. Presumably they didn't want to carry it home in their car where it could tip over and spill, so they'd simply left it on the floor.

For my part, I was now convinced that this bottle of windshield washer liquid was meant for me. So I filled up my car's windshield washer container and propped the bottle containing the remaining liquid upright in my car trunk, wedged in my sports bag.

Amazed at how fate had intervened in such a curious manner, we went into the shopping mall and bought some items of clothing. Laden with shopping, we decided to go back to the car to leave the clothes there before going to the bookshop. On the way back to the car I remarked to Punam that if this windshield washer liquid really had been sent to us, then I wouldn't be surprised to find a cap that fit the bottle.

Sure enough, as I opened my car's trunk, I noticed there was a discarded soda bottle lid under the car next to mine. I really wasn't surprised to find that it fit the bottle of windshield washer liquid perfectly.

Wonderful! Now even more buoyant, we went back into the shopping mall to go into the bookshop.

Because of my recent psychic experiences, I'd taken to

watching a TV show called *Most Haunted*. This featured a team of ghost hunters who would go into various haunted locations at night to see what they could film. I was intrigued by the Spiritualist medium, Derek Acorah, who was with the team. He seemed to pick up all sorts of detailed information about the location he claimed not to have known before. Was the program, in fact, scripted? If not, how did he do it?

I was browsing the Mind, Body, and Spirit section of the bookshop when I noticed a book called *The Psychic World of Derek Acorah*. It was about his life and explained how he worked as a medium. I bought it, took it home, and read it in a few hours.

I was halfway through the book when I happened to take a good look at the cover. It had been written by Derek Acorah with John G. Sutton. It was that name again.

The next day, there was an entry in the house call request book for a patient named Sutton. I'd kept the receptionists at work informed of my strange coincidences and so Carol was adamant: "You've got to go," she said.

Mrs. Sutton was very ancient and had a swollen knee. I got chatting with her daughter Thelma and mentioned my curious Sutton coincidences. Thelma told me she'd had the same experience with the name "Long."

"You know, I don't believe in coincidences," she said. "I think you were meant to come here so I could tell you about my father."

"What about him?" I asked.

"Well, he died four years ago. But one evening he appeared before me as large as life and held my hand. And do you know what? His hand was as warm as yours or mine!"

I told the receptionists what had happened. They all began whistling the Twilight Zone theme.

I felt I had strayed into a whole other realm. I'd spent the past seven years writing computer software. It seemed to me I'd looked up from my computer monitor to find the world had changed around me.

I met Catherine in the gym soon after and told her about what had been happening to me.

"I suppose at least you can see more clearly now," she said, with reference to my clean windshield.

As soon as she said it, I made the symbolic connection that had been nagging at me all the time. Clairvoyance means "clear seeing." Therefore, windshield washer liquid, as a sort of divine gift, was appropriate in this context.

I rather enjoyed these coincidences. I began to see a pattern to them. When I was calm and happy, nothing unusual seemed to happen. I wasn't certain, but they seemed to occur when I was stressed, confused, or looking for direction. When I thought about it, this had happened to me before. One coincidence in particular had occurred to me when I had to choose a medical school. I was 17 and it had set the whole course of my life.

14

Idiot Child!

Being overweight and wearing glasses was a considerable handicap for me as a child. I didn't like physical exercise when I was at school. There were too many associations with competitive games for my taste. Because I was always afraid of getting my glasses broken, I avoided sports such as rugby. Instead, I hung around the school library and soon got a position as a librarian. This was good because it meant I could spend all my breaks between lessons indoors sitting in the library, which prevented me from being beaten up in schoolyard fights. As a bonus, I could do my homework during school hours, so when I got home I could watch TV or read science fiction books all evening.

The downside was Linden Lewington. Linden was a school prefect and six years older than me. Otherwise, in most respects, he was a larger version of myself: overweight and bespectacled. He used to twist my ear and call me "idiot child." He made quite an impression on me.

After a couple of years, Linden left school for university. However, he was subsequently to influence my life so profoundly I can honestly say, if it wasn't for Linden I wouldn't have met my wife. Here's how Linden did it.

In the UK, medicine is an undergraduate course, just like any other degree, though much longer. So I was in my senior year and looking to apply for medical school. I also had a Saturday job with the borough library service. It was boring work, but it gave me the opportunity to have access to lots of science textbooks I wouldn't otherwise have known about.

The library I was based at was quite out of the way in

Muswell Hill. But one Saturday I was transferred to cover for someone at a different library in Wood Green, just for that day. It was there that I came across Linden again. He was doing a temporary job at Wood Green library having just completed a neurosciences degree. He took an interest in my medical school application and asked me which medical schools I'd chosen. I'd settled on Manchester University for my first choice and the Welsh National School of Medicine for my second choice. He suggested I should apply to Nottingham University instead of Manchester; in his opinion it was much better.

I'd looked at the Nottingham University medical course and hadn't really fancied it, probably because the prospectus was quite dull-looking. However, Linden was very enthusiastic about it and mentioned that Nottingham University medical school awarded you an additional science degree after the third year, which wasn't common in those days. He gave me a lift home in his car. As I got out of the car, I remember him leaning across the passenger seat saying, "Make sure you look at Nottingham."

When I got home, I dug out the Nottingham University medical school prospectus and decided he was right. I chose Nottingham as my first choice for medical school and was very lucky to get a place there.

Sometime in the mid-1990s, I popped into our local library to borrow some books. I noticed a portly, graying, middle-aged man who appeared to be with a younger woman. They were queuing to return some books and had a couple of small kids in tow. The man looked for all the world like an older version of Linden.

I whispered to Punam, "I'm sure I know that man," and went up to him.

"Are you Linden Lewington?" I asked.

He visibly paled and backed away a little.

"Yes." His tone was defensive and he eyed me suspiciously.

At this point, I got carried away. I think I said something like this: "My name's Ian Rubenstein and you used to twist my ear and call me idiot child and you told me to go to Nottingham medical school where I met my wife and these are my children so thank you," without drawing breath.

He became even paler and said, "Good Lord! After I told you to go to medical school, I decided to go to medical school as well. I'm now a doctor, too. I'm a specialist in cardiology, my wife's a nurse and these are my children."

It turned out his wife worked at a neighboring medical center just a short distance away from my own.

We all looked at each other in a brief moment of silence. At which point the librarian sitting at the desk in front of us shook her head and said, "I've never heard anything like this before!"

Looking back, I could see the connecting thread was, of course, the library. I've always liked books, but I never expected to find a copy of my own personal Book of Life in the local library.

I met Linden again at a party given by some close friends, one of whom was a health visitor who'd worked with his wife. I had a chance to talk to him and found him much more open to the possibility of meaningful coincidences than I'd expected. He was certainly interested in my psychic experiences.

It seems Linden and I are bound together in some strange way. Maybe that's why he was instrumental in helping me to get to know my first spirit guide. Not that he realized it, of course.

15

Enter the Guides

I'd been attending the psychic development circle for six months. By then I'd become used to the format. Keith Hudson would conduct a guided meditation before we started clairvoyance. The meditation would usually take the form of an imaginary journey. Tonight, however, we were going to go on an imaginary journey with the express intention of meeting our spirit guides. As Keith said this, I had all the usual thoughts and misgivings about what we were really doing. Not that I was worried that what we were doing was dangerous. What really concerned me was how Keith's view of the world and the way it worked clashed with my scientific and medical knowledge. Repeatedly, I wondered who or what these guides really were. Although Spiritualists assumed they were spiritual beings, I had a nagging feeling they could just be parts of my own mind.

Eventually, I would conclude that these distinctions might be merely a limitation of our viewpoint as physical beings. Maybe both views were correct. However, at this stage I had to try to somehow accommodate these two different viewpoints. For the time being, I agreed with myself to buy into the Spiritualist way of seeing things when I was doing psychic work. I could live with that—though rather uncomfortably.

For this evening's exercise, first we were to open up psychically. I went through the procedure of imagining myself anchored to the ground, then bringing the light up through my legs, then my spine, until I could imagine it leaving through the top of my head. I was then fully open.

Keith next instructed us to imagine we were walking along a path. We were to expect to meet someone very special at the end of the path. As usual, he said, "Don't concentrate. Contemplate. Just let it happen. Don't try. Just observe."

I pictured in my mind a grassy pathway. Ahead was a huge tree, which looked like some sort of cedar. The weather was hot but there was shade under the tree. In the background, behind the tree, I could see a low building made of white stone. Bright sunlight reflected off its walls. Under the tree was a stone bench. I sat down on the bench and became aware of a man sitting next to me on my left. He looked to be in his sixties. He was bald, or possibly had shaved his head. He had a short beard and pleasant features. His eyes were pale gray and twinkling. He wore simple gray robes and looked like a monk. I imagined I could hear him speaking to me.

"Hello, Little Brother," he said. "I am Nestor. Do you remember me?"

"Are you my spirit guide?" I asked.

"One of them, yes," he said. This answer surprised me.

"How many guides do I have?" I asked.

"Don't worry about that at the moment. You'll find out in time."

"How long have you been my guide?" I asked.

"All your life," said Nestor. "And I've given you guidance in other lives, too."

"Other lives. So reincarnation is a fact."

"Yes, if you wish."

"That's very cryptic. What do you mean by 'if you wish'?"

Nestor laughed. "You know what I mean. I've shown you."

I'd recently been reading about reincarnation. I'd never much liked the thought of it, but as my wife and her family were practicing Hindus, I couldn't really escape from considering the concept. I wanted to see how it fit in with what I was learning about in my psychic development circle.

The straightforward Hindu notion is that we are each a

soul, which goes through cycles of birth-death-rebirth. We carry experiences from each life with us and work off or accumulate moral debt as the cycle continues. But that was just one way of looking at it.

I'd also been reading about the Buddhist view of reincarnation. This is more sophisticated. Buddhists believe that nothing actually reincarnates because individuality is an illusion and nothing is constant, not even the physical self from one moment to another. In this view, an individual conscious being is like a wave that appears briefly on a huge ocean of universal consciousness. The ocean is constant but one wave creates another and so on. There is a link between the waves, but there is no constant individual soul that reincarnates.

I'd been thinking about this one day when I had a realization, which came to me seemingly out of the blue. I experienced the mental image of a huge, multi-faceted diamond. Light was shining through the diamond. I could see that the diamond represented a human soul. Each facet of the diamond represented one lifetime. I realized that time as we experience it on Earth is merely an illusion due to our current perspective. The diamond exists, has existed, and will always exist in a sort of timeless state.

I could see that the purpose of life was to polish each facet. We say life grinds us down. A diamond in a jewelry workshop could make the same complaint. In fact, the grinding polishes our facets, to add beauty and harmony to the whole gem.

Perhaps "I" as I experienced myself in each life, am merely one aspect of the whole diamond, and a very limited aspect at that. As a mere facet I am flat compared with the three-dimensional nature of the whole diamond. The whole diamond would be my "higher self." Then suppose each diamond was stacked together with others. Perhaps each whole diamond in its own way represented a single facet of an even greater diamond, a huge structure, which kept on stacking up until what? God?

I was quite pleased with this thought but I'd begun to suspect it wasn't entirely my own. I began to come across similar concepts in various books I was reading. Had I read about it before and assumed it was my own idea? I didn't think so. Now this spirit guide was saying he'd shown the whole thing to me!

"Thank you for that, Nestor. It seems I don't have an original idea in my head. I thought I was so clever."

"Little Brother," he said, "you will discover the true nature of knowledge in due course. But now I would like to show you some of your past life when we were on Earth together."

He showed me in an instant. It was as if someone had dropped a parcel of information into my mind. I knew what was in the parcel even though I had yet to unwrap it.

He showed me a life where I was someone completely different. We were living in a monastery. I realized it was a Nestorian monastery—not that I knew what a Nestorian monastery was. I knew it was somewhere with a hot climate. The monastery was very cool inside. Its architecture was simpler, somehow rougher than, and not in the style I would usually associate with, a European monastery.

My guide was the head of the order: I suppose he'd have been the abbot. I was one of the monks with an administrative role. He showed me I'd been a very persnickety, ordered sort of individual, someone who was much at home with books, forms, requests; in other words, I'd been a bit of a bureaucrat.

Then he drew my attention to something else. Ever since I was very small, I'd always been interested in office equipment. Staplers, card indexes, typewriters—you name it, I just loved it. Even now, I can happily spend time flicking through office equipment catalogs. My interest in computers stems from the fact that I had no fear of keyboards because I taught myself to type when I was 13 years old. Although I can be slapdash, I also have the capacity for very painstaking, detailed work. Writing computer software involves the minutest attention to detail. I always wondered where that had come from.

"These aspects of your personality have come under the influence of the life I am showing you. In a sense, they came from this life," explained Nestor.

What a load of nonsense, I thought. You couldn't make this stuff up.

I could sense a gentle chuckle from Nestor. "Precisely. You aren't making this up. You would have done anything to obtain such items in my day."

Could I believe this? Does one choose a life just because there's loads of cool office equipment to play with?

"When was your day, exactly?" I asked. I didn't hear Nestor say anything, but I just knew it was about the eighth or ninth century.

Then that was it; it was over. My meditation abruptly terminated, and I was back in the dimly lit church hall, sitting in the circle. The others still had their eyes closed.

I didn't know what to make of it. At last, I'd finally met my guide. Or perhaps it was a bit of me that thought it was my guide. I was, if anything, more perplexed than before.

The others finished their meditations. As usual, Keith asked each of us in turn to describe what we'd seen. Some people had had difficulty visualizing anything. Others had met guides who were very familiar to them.

When it was my turn, I was hesitant.

"Well, I met a guide, or perhaps I met a part of myself, or perhaps it was just my imagination. Anyway, he's a monk and he said he was Nestor."

Jeff was indignant. "For God's sake, Doc! You met your guide. Stop all this rubbish about you're not sure if it's this or that. Just take it! You're driving us all mad."

"That's because he's a doctor," said Keith. "He's too educated. It's good to question. But sometimes you just have to accept things first. You'll get the answers afterwards."

People were smiling and shaking their heads. I realized they actually felt sorry for me. They could see how difficult it was for me to fit these ideas into my way of thinking. My education was proving to be a real handicap. I couldn't just accept things as they were given to me.

"Well, anyway," I said. "I'm not sure if his name actually is Nestor. That's the name he used, but I think it's just because he was a Nestorian monk."

Keith nodded in patient agreement. "Names don't mean a lot over there. They'll often take a name just because it has a meaning for you. Don't worry about it. It took ages before my guide told me his name."

I told him about my supposed former life in a monastery. No eyebrows were raised. Some people nodded sagely. I decided to keep the part about office equipment to myself. That was just too bizarre.

I still found the concept of a personal spirit guide very difficult to swallow. I could cope with the idea that I had a higher self, but not that there would be someone assigned to me personally. Wouldn't they get bored? Of course, I'd read about spirit guides and guardian angels, but I'd never given them much thought. Now, how was I going to deal with this?

Not very easily, as it turned out. I was comfortable with the idea that our consciousness may not be what it seems, that we may have hidden powers that may be responsible for meaningful coincidences and the occurrence of strange events. I could just about accept that when people die some part of them might continue, which at least raised the possibility of after-death communication. Sure, I had my doubts, who wouldn't?

However, when it came to the idea that we may each have a personal guide or guardian angel, well, that was a different matter. I baulked at that because I knew how easy it was to fool yourself. I'd used hypnosis clinically for many years and I knew just how incredible the human mind could be. This could all simply be an elaborate fantasy. I'd suspended my disbelief so far. But how far was I really prepared to go? If I accepted the concept of spirit guides, what then? It opened the possibility of there being whole classes of discarnate beings. On the other hand, if humans genuinely did survive death, then why not? Perhaps there really was a whole universe out there we just hadn't noticed.

As usual, I demanded proof. And as usual, I received proof in a way I found hard to ignore. I found it hard to ignore because it involved Linden. And whenever anything happens to me involving Linden, it involves a library. This tells me it's a put-up job.

It happened two days after the meditation in which I'd met my guide. I was in the local library choosing some books, but I gradually began to feel an insistent tugging at the back of my mind. It's hard to describe the feeling. I tried to dismiss it but the sensation became stronger and stronger. I found I couldn't concentrate on the books I was looking at. I felt I had to get out of the library because I had an important meeting. But I knew I hadn't scheduled any meetings for that day as it was a Saturday.

The feeling grew stronger and, as I tried to ignore it, I could almost hear a voice saying, "Come on, you'll be late for your meeting."

I realized it was Nestor. I couldn't see him, but I could feel his presence.

"You're me, aren't you?" I said to myself.

"No, I'm Nestor, your guide. Please don't be late for your meeting."

Okay, I thought, I'll play along with this.

"What do you want me to do?" I said, possibly to myself.

"Leave the library, go and buy the sunglasses you wanted. Then go to the drugstore."

I'd not yet chosen any books, but I hurried out of the library and bought a pair of sunglasses.

I didn't need anything from the drugstore and felt slightly stupid for going there, but I thought I'd see where this led me.

It was a busy day in Boots' drugstore. I didn't have a clue why I was there. I stood in the center of the shop for a few seconds looking perplexed. I then realized I knew the couple standing in front of me. It was Linden and his wife, Kay. I approached them in a state of some excitement.

"I knew you'd be here. Well, actually, I didn't know it would be you, but as it happened in a library I should have guessed..."

Linden and Kay looked at each other.

"My spirit guide told me to come here," I finished, somewhat lamely.

"Really," said Linden, possibly trying to humor me. "I wonder why?"

"I suppose it was to meet you. To let me know he's real?"

"Your spirit guide," repeated Linden. His wife looked at him, nervously.

"Yes. Well, it's completely nuts isn't it? Good to see you two. Bye!"

I turned and left. I didn't know whether to feel embarrassed or elated.

As usual, the doubts started to surface once again. How did I know it wasn't just me all along?

Worse was yet to come.

16

Any Friend of Lara Croft is a Friend of Mine

I was sitting at my desk about to start my morning clinic when I became aware of a voice. The voice was definitely inside my mind, but there was a sense of presence to it. It was as if someone was standing behind me and leaning forward.

"I am Kosa," said the voice. It sounded African. I'd heard the accent somewhere before but I couldn't place it. I received a powerful visual impression of a tall, gangling, young African man. He was smiling broadly, showing perfect white teeth. He was wearing colored beads from around the lower part of his legs to just above his ankles.

By this time, I'd become used to such matters, so I stopped what I was doing and carried on a little internal conversation.

"Who are you, Kosa?" I asked

"I am your new guide," he said.

"That's an interesting name. I've never heard of it before. Where is it from?"

"South Africa," he said.

I didn't know how to spell the name, so I entered it into Google using "Kosa" and "South Africa" as the search terms. I didn't get much with the spelling KOSA but one web-page revealed that the correct spelling of Kosa was XHOSA. The Xhosa people are a major South African ethnic group. You may have heard of Nelson Mandela—he's a Xhosa.

Another major South African ethnic group is, of course, the Zulu people. I remembered reading that Zulu spirit guides were known as spiritual powerhouses because they were often used to provide the energy for spirit communication. So I didn't have a Zulu as a guide; instead, I had a Xhosa. Well, if it was good enough for Nelson Mandela, then it was certainly good enough for me.

"But hang on Xhosa, if that's your ethnic name, what's your real name?" I asked.

"Just call me Kosa," was all he said. Then I received an image of a young European man with long, straight, straggly hair wearing a loose, long-sleeved shirt. Standing next to him was the tall, thin African man dressed in old-fashioned naval uniform on the deck of a fully-rigged sailing ship. It seemed Kosa and I were old friends; he was showing me we knew each other from a previous life. There was nothing else. Someone had turned off my mental TV set.

Disconcertingly, I heard him again while driving back from the morning's house calls for my afternoon clinic.

"Ian, it is me, Kosa."

"Hello, Kosa, or whoever you are."

"Ian, I want to prove to you I am real. You know you need a new cartridge for your ink-jet printer?"

"Yes. What about it?"

"Now would be a good time to go and buy one. You can stop off at PC World."

"No, I can't. I'll be late for my clinic."

"Ian, it would be a real shame if you didn't go to PC World now."

I mentally shrugged my shoulders and went with it. Usually the computer store was crowded and you would have to queue for ages at the check-out. This time, however, it was empty and there was no queue. I found my ink-jet cartridge and went to pay. To my great surprise, one of my patients was at the register.

"Hello, Pauline," I said. "I didn't know you worked here."

"I don't usually work the register, but we've got staff off sick so I've got to cover. Lucky it's quiet today." She looked at my purchase and winked at me. "I'll put that on my staff discount—20 percent off."

In my head I heard an African accented voice chuckling.

On my way out, I mentally thanked Kosa. "I wasn't aware spirit guides take such an interest in modern technology."

"The whole point was to show you I'm real. We'll be working together."

"But how do I know you aren't just a sort of secondary personality? Maybe you're really a bit of me I've created—something I can allow to access my own psychic powers...I don't know."

There was no reply. Perhaps he'd gone off in a huff.

Despite my detour, I wasn't late for my clinic.

My philosophical stumbling block was giving me a headache. If I was beginning to interact with internal voices, I desperately needed to decide what I was about. What did I believe?

I wished I could stop thinking and analyzing. The chief problem, as I saw it, was the reality or otherwise of my spirit guides. I knew that having made contact with my guides I was supposed to develop a working relationship with them. As far as Spiritualists are concerned, mediums need to work with their spirit guides to become even half-decent at what they do.

This would have been fun but for my nagging doubts. Was I sure this wasn't just a part of me? Was I kidding myself?

Sitting in circle one evening, I became aware of Kosa. I hadn't had any contact with him in circle before. Kosa announced himself by showing me a mental picture of his legs: bare feet with colored beads tied around his ankles. He came across as young, fairly inexperienced, but very energetic.

I'd been having a bad day. I was tired and quite frankly couldn't be bothered. I issued a mental challenge to Kosa. "Listen, if you're real, then you can do it all tonight. I'm not even going to try. I just haven't got the energy."

I sat back in my chair. The church hall was only dimly illuminated by the flickering candle Keith Hudson had placed on the floor in the center of the circle. I contemplated and let my mind go.

I saw, or imagined I saw, a sort of dark, double silhouette that moved into the circle from my right to my left. It hovered in front of Dave, a member of the group I hadn't met before. As I looked, it resolved itself into two people.

They were an elderly couple, both of short stature. The man was wearing working clothes and a leather apron. We had a kind of internal dialogue. He told me he was Dave's grandfather. His name was Frank and he'd brought along his wife, whose name was Elizabeth. He showed me his old workshop. I could see a workbench on top of which were many pieces of folded leather and some small, wooden-handled brass tools. He told me he'd died 30 years before.

"What message do you want me to give to Dave?" I asked, in my mind.

"Tell him he's lost something. If he keeps on searching, it will turn up."

I passed the message on. Dave was a rather quiet and unassuming middle-aged man who looked like he often found life quite painful. His unenthusiastic response to my message left me feeling discouraged for the rest of the session. By the time we'd finished, I really felt I'd failed miserably and I wondered why I'd bothered to come that evening.

As we were leaving, I approached Dave and asked him what he thought about the message I'd given him: "It's my first proper message really. Did it mean anything to you?"

Dave smiled at me, shyly.

"Oh, yes. That was definitely my grandfather," he said.

I was shocked. "Was it really?"

Dave seemed surprised at my reaction. This was his first time in circle. He'd simply assumed I was a medium and did this all the time. When I told him I was new to this, he confirmed his grandfather's name had been Frank and his grandmother's had been Elizabeth. Frank had worked as a bookbinder, specializing in leather bindings. I had accurately described his workshop, even down to the little tools he used. They had indeed both died 30 years before.

"So what have you lost, then?" I asked.

"I lost the keys to the factory where I work. I can't find them anywhere. I wish he'd told you where I should look for them."

My mood changed from one of dejection to exhilaration. I'd completely misjudged Dave's reaction to my message. This feeling didn't last long though, because again I had to confront the reality or otherwise of spirit guides.

I was at home one evening soon after I'd given the surprisingly accurate message to Dave. It was late and everyone had gone to bed. I didn't feel tired and was listlessly flicking through the TV channels but there was nothing worth watching. My younger son, Paul, had recorded a video some months before. The tape was sitting on the shelf under the TV. I looked at the label. There was writing crossed through from previous recordings but this recording looked like *Lara Croft and the Cradle of Life*. Idly, I wondered what it was about. I pushed the cassette into the video recorder and pressed play.

It was definitely a film for kids with Angelina Jolie in the lead role as Lara Croft, a sort of female Indiana Jones. I lost track of it halfway through and started to think about the strange things I'd experienced recently.

In particular, I returned to wondering about the true nature of guides. Were my guides real? Were they figments of my imagination? If they were real, what would it be like to be a guide and to have to hang around someone all the time? Personally, I wouldn't much fancy having to do that. I'd probably get bored. None of this made sense.

And who is this Kosa character? I thought.

Then Angelina Jolie, as Lara Croft on the TV, said, "Ask Kosa to meet me."

What was that? I could have sworn I'd just heard Angelina Jolie mention Kosa.

I paused the video recording and wound the tape back a little. The Lara Croft character was on the telephone talking to someone about going to Kilimanjaro.

"Ask Kosa to meet me north of his village," said Lara Croft.

That got my attention. I watched the rest of the video, transfixed. Kosa turned out to be her African guide who had to lead Lara Croft across the plains of Kilimanjaro, fighting off evil spirits on the way.

I fancied I could hear a little chuckle in my head.

But how can this be? I thought. This is schizophrenia! Seeing things on TV I feel have a personal message for me! It's madness!

I replayed the tape. It was still there! Go away!

What were the chances I would be thinking about my African spirit guide, supposedly named Kosa, at the same time I was watching a movie that happened to feature an African guide, also named Kosa?

Maybe I'd heard about Kosa before. Maybe I'd gotten the name from the movie. I checked the next day. Paul had recorded it in January but hadn't bothered to watch it. None of us had ever seen the film before. The movie hadn't introduced the Kosa character up to the point where I'd heard the name mentioned. I'd never played video games and I wasn't familiar with the Tomb Raider games from which the Lara Croft character originated.

Naturally, I mentioned this at the psychic development circle.

"Yes, they can do that," said Keith Hudson, matter-of-factly.

I didn't know what to say. "Yes, they can do that" implied that just about everything I thought of in life as true was in fact a mere sham.

"Yes, they can do that" meant somehow my son could record a tape containing a message for me, before I'd even begun to attend the psychic development circle. How could "they" arrange events in such a way so that at the exact moment I would be thinking about my guide Kosa, I would happen to see the same thing on TV? An African guide named Kosa who was fighting off evil spirits no less!

Alternatively, it could have been just a coincidence. That's what most scientifically educated people would say. Indeed, it was a coincidence: the events coincided, certainly. Nevertheless, somehow they seemed to be linked. And however much I tried to dismiss this, it just seemed blindingly obvious that somehow it had all been arranged—for my benefit.

How?

For the time being, I just had to accept that...yes, they can do that.

17

Don't I Know Your Father?

Ireland in August 2004 was beautiful. We were on vacation and staying in a cottage in a peaceful village. The cottage was comfortable and the local pub served great food. There was also a small stone circle close by and an ancient holy well just outside the village on the main road.

I visited both the stone circle and the holy well and attempted to open my psychic senses, but I wasn't convinced I could pick up anything at all. We had a better result at the pub where we picked up a good meal for a very reasonable sum.

When weird things happen, they usually occur when you least expect them. Midway through our trip to Ireland we decided to go for a long walk. The footpath we chose would take us through woodland above a bay and down to a small coastal village. We'd allowed a whole day for this and planned to stop off at a pub somewhere for lunch.

While we were walking in the woods, I began to get the strangest feeling. It was a warm day and the air was heavy and full of the sound of buzzing wasps. This was a slightly menacing noise, as if we weren't really welcome there. But listening to it somehow enabled me to tune in to something. I experienced a feeling of heavy expectation. It was the sort of feeling I always associate with an imminent thunderstorm. It was as if all my senses were straining.

"I feel strange," I said to my family. "Something's going to happen. I can feel it."

The boys burst into laughter. Dad was being crazy again. The feeling didn't leave me. However, nothing obviously out of the ordinary seemed to be happening. After a couple of hours, we reached the coastal village. Despite its small size, the village had several pubs. We selected the best-looking one and went in to have our lunch. The pub was decorated in traditional style with dark oak decor and fishing paraphernalia hanging on the walls. The bartender was pulling a pint of dark stout while speaking to his only customer, who was propping up the bar in front of him.

We were looking at the lunchtime menu chalked up on a blackboard on the wall and trying to decide which table to sit at. All the while, I had the sensation that "something's going to happen" and I was feeling, well, not anxious, but tense and expectant.

"Look," I said to Punam. "You choose something from the menu. I'll just pop out and have a nose around outside. I've still got that feeling. It won't go away."

The boys started giggling and Punam gave me a withering look. "Don't be long," she said.

I went outside into the narrow, cobbled street. There were just the usual shops: a newsstand and a couple of small gift shops catering to the tourist trade, nothing out of the ordinary. I quickly returned, sat down and placed my order for lunch.

While we were eating, I overheard the conversation between the bartender and his customer at the bar.

The bartender was giving directions. "You go around the M25, get off at junction 24, then go down the A105 and then the A110 to Enfield Town."

I looked at Punam. "Did you hear what he just said?"
"Yes."
"So, he did mention Enfield Town, then?"
"I'm sure he did," agreed Punam.
I raised a finger and waggled it at her.
"That's weird enough for me," I said.
I wondered what the chances were of going hundreds of

miles away to Ireland to overhear a conversation between two strangers giving directions to the place where I lived.

"I've got to ask him," I said.

Punam sighed resignedly. "I suppose you have to."

Meanwhile, Joshua and Paul were nudging me, saying, "Go on Dad, go and ask him. Go on! Go on!"

I got up and made my way to the bar. I caught the bartender's eye and ordered some more drinks.

As he was pouring them, I said, "I couldn't help overhearing what you were saying. I'm a primary care physician and I live in Enfield. I wondered what your connection with the area was."

Very proudly, he explained that his son was a teacher who'd just received a position at one of the high schools very close to where I lived. As he said this, I became certain that his son was my patient and that somehow I had to help him.

"I wonder if he's a patient at our practice. What's his name?" I asked.

The bartender told me his son's name. We exchanged a few pleasantries and I sat back down with the drinks. The expectant feeling had dissipated.

"Have you got your cell phone with you?" I asked Punam.

"Yes. Why?"

"I've got to phone the clinic. I bet he's one of my patients."

Punam looked at me and said, very firmly, "If he's one of your patients, then that's the last thing you need to do. You're on vacation. Check it out when you're back at work."

"I suppose you're right," I said, reluctantly.

We got back to our rented cottage late that afternoon. Punam went off for a shower while the boys went swimming. I looked at the telephone. I'd promised not to phone the clinic, but I really wanted to know. I picked up the telephone and made the call. One of the receptionists answered.

"Sally, I want you to see if we have this patient registered with us."

I gave her his name and address. I heard her typing the details into the computer.

"Nope, nothing," she said.

I was surprised. "Oh. Okay, thanks. See you next week."

"Next week? Aren't you coming in before then?"

"No. I'm on vacation in Ireland."

"If you're on vacation, why are you phoning in about patients?"

"That's a very good question," I said, and put the phone down.

How strange, I thought. A big build up, a teasing coincidence and then...a bit of a damp squib.

Punam came downstairs drying her hair.

"I phoned the clinic," I admitted.

"Ian! You're supposed to be on vacation." She raised her eyebrows. "Well? Is he registered with you?"

"No."

"Never mind. I hope you're not too disappointed."

When we got back to London, I mentioned this coincidence to the other members of the psychic development circle. They agreed that it would have been great if he'd been my patient, but were still impressed with the fact that I'd felt something brewing.

The following night I was busy at the computer in the bedroom we used as a study. I was still writing computer code for my software project, though much less intensively than I had been a few months before. Punam had just finished working a Wednesday evening clinic session. She didn't usually work this particular clinic but was covering a colleague who was on vacation. It was about ten o'clock at night when she got back home. I heard her come upstairs and stride purposefully into the study.

"Ian, I've got something to tell you."

I wasn't interested. I was up to my neck wrestling with a nasty bug in my computer program.

"Tell me later, eh?"

Punam placed a hand on my shoulder. I turned around. She was grinning from ear to ear. Oh, this looked interesting! I sighed and leaned back in my chair.

"Okay. What happened?"

She sat down on the edge of the bed and leaned towards me. Usually calm, she was in a peculiarly animated state.

"Ian, I don't know how to say this. I hardly ever do clinic sessions on Wednesdays, do I? Anyway, I always check the patient's physician's address and with my first patient I noticed he didn't have one locally. When I asked him why, he told me he was from the village in Ireland where we had lunch in that pub. When I checked his name, I was amazed to see that he had the same name as the bartender's son. Guess what? It was him!"

"What!" I exclaimed. "What did you say to him?"

"Well, I just said I thought we'd met his father last week. He told me he'd spoken to him on the phone recently and his dad had mentioned he'd met a couple of doctors from Enfield."

We looked at each other. My hunch had been almost right: he was destined to be a patient, but it would fall to my wife to help him.

"Bloody hell!" I said.

"So what's all this about, then?" I asked Keith Hudson at the next meeting.

Keith gave one of his snorting laughs. "Oh, they're just letting you know they're around. They do this sort of thing."

"Yes, but how? I'd planned that vacation over a year ago. I wasn't even into all this stuff then..."

Keith took a long drag from his cigarette, exhaled the smoke slowly, thoughtfully, and then shrugged his shoulders. "I don't know *how* they do it but they can do this sort of thing. That's how they work. You'll get used to it."

18

Getting Physical

One evening at the end of a Thursday meeting, Keith Hudson took me aside. "Every Tuesday evening we have a physical circle. It's a closed circle. If it's an open circle, anyone can join. You have to be invited to join a closed circle. Anyway, would you like to join us?"

Keith explained that a physical circle was more typical of what most people would think of as a classical Spiritualist séance. It was more formal, attendance was by invitation of the whole group, and it meant a commitment to attend every week. The purpose of a physical circle was to see if a group of people could experience physical phenomena such as the movement of objects, hearing objective voices from the spirit world, even, perhaps, materializations.

Keith felt I had a lot of energy to contribute. He wondered if my sister and I had witnessed Felicity's transfiguration because we'd unwittingly provided the energy to allow it to happen.

The opportunity to observe the same sort of phenomena I'd seen all those years ago was too good to miss.

"I'll be there," I said.

The physical circle was held in a tiny room known as the snug. The sliding door to the snug was always closed when I walked past it on my way into the church every Tuesday evening, and I would hear recorded music coming from the unoccupied room.

"It raises the room's vibrations," explained Keith, when I asked him the reason for the music.

There were seven of us, including Keith, of course, and

me. The other members attending the physical circle were June, a smartly-dressed widow in her fifties who worked as a seamstress and chaired the church services; Jack and Samantha, a married couple in their early thirties, both trainee healers; and Jeff, who was also training to be a healer. I knew them all from the Thursday open circle.

There was also Sagi Bob, an old friend of Keith's who didn't attend the open circle. I asked why he was known as Sagi Bob. I was told that, on account of there being three Bobs in the church, each Bob had been given a unique designation.

Sagi Bob had been born under the sign of Sagittarius. Reiki Bob was a Reiki healer who had decided to learn about spiritual healing. Secret Bob had earned his appellation by often claiming to have received messages from the spirit world but usually refusing to divulge what they were. This made the whole exercise somewhat pointless but perhaps made him feel he'd got one-up on the others.

Sagi Bob was a humorous, forty-something ex-army warehouse worker. He claimed to have seen spirits since he was a child. Apparently he'd experienced difficulties because he hadn't realized no one else could see them.

The group had been sitting in circle for a couple of years. Had they witnessed any physical phenomena? Not at all. Apparently it could take years of patient sitting to get anything. What it involved was sitting in the dark for an hour. Physical circles are usually conducted in the dark. It seems light interferes with the process, which many skeptics find a little too convenient. But at least it was an hour spent with absolutely nothing to do, which in my busy life was a rare luxury. I was up for it.

The snug was small and windowless, about 8 feet by 6 feet. Seven chairs lined the walls. In the center of the room was a small collapsible card table covered with a paper tablecloth.

In the center of the table Keith would place a tall, hollow cone made of aluminum. Looking something like a Victorian speaking trumpet or megaphone, it was open at both ends and known simply as "the trumpet." It had been decorated with a band of luminous paint around its wider base and another around its narrower top. Keith would also arrange on the table a small hand bell and four different-shaped quartz crystals. These were placed around the base of the trumpet. Every object on the table had had its outline very carefully drawn around it in ballpoint pen. This allowed each one to be placed in exactly the same position every week, the principle being that if any of the objects moved during the séance it would be obvious afterwards once the lights were turned back on. There would also be two round plastic tea trays placed on the floor beneath the table. They'd been painted with the same luminous paint that adorned the trumpet.

Jeff always carried a washing-up bowl of water into the snug, which he placed on the floor in one corner of the room. June would hand around a tray of glass beer mugs containing water for people to drink. When I asked what all the water was for, Keith explained that water was very important for physical phenomena because "it's a good conductor."

Physical circles are quite rare nowadays. In the early years of the twentieth century they were much more common, and they often claimed to have produced many types of physical phenomena. Opinions differ as to why physical phenomena are rarer today.

Skeptics say we are today much more sophisticated and aware of fraud, so it's harder to get away with it. Believers say the problem is society has changed. People wishing to experience physical phenomena have to sit together, often for many years, in order to establish a good rapport before physical phenomena begin. That was fine in the old days when people had no other entertainment at home. Today we are much busier in our lives with less time for socializing, preferring instead an evening in front of the TV. Also, perhaps there was more need for the Other Side to provide physical evidence in the past because of the number of losses in the two world wars.

Each week we'd sit in the snug and turn out the lights. Keith would say a brief opening prayer for protection, and we would then open ourselves up psychically. The room would be lit only by the faint, eerie glow of the luminous paint on the trays and the trumpet.

How much fun can you have sitting in the dark with a bunch of people you've only known for a few months? The answer is—an enormous amount.

Firstly, there's the sheer adolescent deliciousness of it all: hey, we're sitting in the dark trying to contact the "Other Side." Who knows what will happen?

Secondly, there were the stories. Keith Hudson was not your average Spiritualist medium. He was an extremely well-read, pleasantly eccentric chain-smoker who loved old books and used to run a couple of New Age bookshops in Walthamstow. Now in his sixties, he'd never married. He was happy in his one-room apartment, enjoyed a pint and quiz-nights at his local pub, and liked an occasional card game with Colin, his landlord. When not giving psychic readings to people, he was happiest browsing around charity shops looking for secondhand books at bargain prices. Keith had been a medium for more than 30 years. Consequently, he was well-known in the Spiritualist movement throughout much of South East England. If you wanted the low-down on what had happened, was happening and (with his clairvoyant powers) would happen—he was the guy to listen to.

People often accuse Spiritualists, and mediums in particular, of being credulous. They've obviously never listened to a bunch of them gossiping. There's always a certain amount of one-upmanship going on. If there's a whiff of fraud or scandalous conduct, they'll be on to it in an instant.

Keith knew about, and often knew personally, many of the most famous mediums of the 1970s, '80s, and '90s. Undoubtedly, the most famous medium he'd ever sat with was Leslie Flint. Leslie Flint gave messages using independent direct voice. When he was sitting in séance, instead of going into a trance or receiving mental messages, voices would talk out of thin air. Although this is very hard to believe, nonetheless investigators had never detected fraud. Keith was convinced that at one séance he'd spoken to an old work colleague who'd died several years previously.

It would have been great if voices started speaking out of thin air in our circle. However, more realistically, we hoped we might observe some light phenomena, such as flashes or balls of light floating in the air, or the movement of some of our test objects on the table.

Most weeks, we'd just sit in the dark and chat, while Jeff and Jack went off into a trance or possibly just fell asleep. At the end of the session, we'd discuss what they'd experienced. When we weren't chatting, I would frequently experience powerful mental images. Surprisingly, these images usually seemed to relate to whatever Samantha, who was a nursery nurse, had been doing at work that day.

For example, one evening I found myself visualizing a circus train. There were all sorts of animals in cages. The peculiar thing was the animals were waving at me. I mentioned this bizarre image to the others. That day, Samantha had been reading the children a story from a picture book, which contained the very same image as an illustration. Incidents like this happened so often in the circle they became commonplace and hardly worth mentioning.

Once, while sitting silently in the dark, we heard a strange quacking noise.

"What's that?" asked June.

Two quacks. Then silence.

"Can't you hear it?" she asked.

Another two quacks.

"I don't think it's coming from the room," said Keith.

"No," said June. "Is there something in the corridor?"

There were then three quacks in quick succession.

"Oh. I know what that is," said Jack.

"Not the spirit of the duck from the Chinese takeout we had last night?" asked Samantha.

"It's you, isn't it Bob?" said Jack.

Bob tried to sound nonchalant. "What do you mean?"

"It's a farting machine," said Jack. "I used to have one when I was a kid. I know that sound."

Bob came clean. He had a remotely controlled farting machine with nine different easily selectable farting sounds; just the thing to break the ice at parties. He couldn't resist it.

We still meet every Tuesday. We think a crystal moved once, but we're not sure...Bob could have shoved the table.

19

Suburban Shaman

When I first started attending the psychic development circle, it was very difficult for me to learn how to still my mind, open up, and try to receive information psychically. So when Keith used to say, "It's so lovely to close down and have a rest," I found it hard to understand what he meant. I soon found out.

It first happened when I was consulting with a disabled patient of mine who'd come with her caregiver. I couldn't help feeling I was being directed to address her caregiver. I would stop speaking to my patient in mid-sentence and turn towards the caregiver as if I were about to say something to her. But then I'd frown, shake my head, and turn back to my patient. It was obvious from the glances exchanged between them they were finding my behavior very strange.

Eventually I put my pen down on my desk and turned to look at the caregiver directly. I felt I had something to tell her. If I didn't speak to her about it, I knew I wasn't going to get anywhere with this consultation.

"Excuse me," I said.

She looked at me quizzically.

"Have you lost anyone recently?" I asked, hesitantly. I had the strangest impression: she'd lost her mother or, at least, someone like her mother. "Look, has your mother died recently?"

"Sort of—yes," she said. "I looked after a lady who died a week ago. She was like a mother to me. How did you know that?"

I fudged it. "Oh, I don't know. I get these odd notions now and again."

Suddenly, I could see in my mind's eye a gray Siamese cat with a bell collar around its neck.

"Did she have a cat? Gray Siamese?" I asked, without any more explanation.

"Yes. As a matter of fact, she did."

I was really enjoying myself now.

"Tell me, why am I also seeing purple ribbons?" I asked, because I now had an image of purple ribbons being wound around something.

"I did the flowers for her funeral," explained the caregiver. "I wound purple ribbons around the flowers."

My disabled patient was looking at me very peculiarly.

"You must be psychic," she said, quite matter-of-factly.

Now I made the mistake of trying to get more...and lost whatever connection I had.

They both took the message remarkably well.

The caregiver even said to me, "Thank you for telling me what you were sensing. I'll always feel she's around me now," as they left.

As the door closed behind them I felt exhilarated but completely drained and a little confused. This wasn't what I'd expected. While I'd given my German patient, Elli, a message she could take, I felt it had really been down to Maureen from the circle rather than me. Furthermore, I had a very good relationship with Elli. In this case, though, I'd felt compelled to give a message to a complete stranger. I'd never met either of these women before. Suppose I'd said something they didn't like and then they'd complained to the authorities. I wanted to nip this in the bud, but at the same time I was intrigued. Thinking about it, I realized I was in the perfect position to give messages from departed relatives. This was serious stuff. If it was going to impact upon my work, then I had to give it some serious thought. What should I do—play safe or push the boat out?

It happened again a couple of days later.

Gordon had died about a month before. He'd been in his late seventies and his health had deteriorated quite rapidly. I was seeing Jacqueline, his daughter-in-law, primarily for bereavement counseling.

While we were talking, I had a vivid image of Gordon wearing a hat with antlers and a comical expression on his face.

This time I was going to be a bit clever.

"You know what?" I said to Jacqueline. "Whenever I think of Gordon, I can't help imagining he's up there in heaven. In fact, I can see him sitting in some medieval wooden hall on a wooden chair like a throne, with antlers over his head."

Her reaction was surprisingly normal.

"Oh. So, you've seen the photo, then. When did he show it to you?"

"What photo?" I asked.

"So, you haven't seen it? It's just that about 20 years ago he was an extra in a comedy film. He had to wear a funny hat, which had these enormous antlers sticking out of it and carry a shotgun. They gave him a photo. I thought he'd shown it to you."

I'd never seen the photograph. I'd only come to know Gordon well during his final illness, and he'd been much too ill to be showing off.

"No, I never knew that," I said. "Funny, isn't it? Maybe that's Gordon letting us know he's there."

Jacqueline gave me a knowing look, but didn't discuss it further.

A few weeks later, I was with Margaret, a visually impaired woman in her seventies. Her husband, Ted, had died a couple of months before. I knew Margaret very well and felt comfortable enough to be completely open with her.

She was very interested in my stories and asked me if I could sense anything around her. I was hoping she would. I put out some mental feelers and, sure enough, I could sense Ted's presence. It's hard to say how I sensed him, but I could tell he was there. My mind was filled with images of their courting days, when he would meet her in the West End of London. I also had images of the war cemeteries they used to visit in their caravan. It flowed very easily. Margaret was convinced I'd made contact with Ted. As ever, I was more skeptical.

"Maybe I'm just reading your mind," I cautioned.

Just reading her mind! I'd come a long way if I now thought that telepathy was something commonplace.

Then Ted was there. It wasn't like seeing him with my eyes, but more vivid than just my imagination.

I could see him standing in front of the door to my room. He looked well and had a broad grin on his face. He was carrying a bundle of blankets under his left arm. He didn't say anything but was pointing to the blankets with his right hand and then gesturing to Margaret. This meant very little to me, so I told Margaret what I was seeing.

Very calmly, she said, "He's telling me to make sure I take his blankets to the hospice. I promised him I'd do it, but I haven't got around to it yet."

The atmosphere in my office had become extremely pleasant and tranquil. Margaret was very pleased with what I'd told her and gave me a kiss. I felt elated but I also found I was feeling quite tired.

Never shy about coming forward, I told my colleagues at the medical center what I was doing. I must be a very lucky man. They expressed their misgivings but were remarkably supportive, especially considering two of them were very devout Christians who didn't really approve of anything purporting to be communication from the spirit world. I was told to be careful, not just because of my career, but also because possibly my soul was in danger.

I very much doubted my soul was in danger. The chief danger was fatigue. Whatever I was doing, it seemed to require a lot of energy and made me very tired. Keith warned me about this.

"You shouldn't be doing this in clinic. You'll wear yourself out," he said.

"Maybe," I said. "But it's so helpful."

Indeed it was. My patients loved it. I don't think I'd ever had so many hugs in my life. As I was discovering, my patients were much more open to this kind of thing than I'd suspected. In fact, once they found out my interest, they started to tell me about their own psychic experiences.

I realized that, as a doctor, I had a very blinkered view of the world. It occurred to me that for years I'd assumed my patients thought in more or less the same way as I did. Sure, I was perhaps better informed than they were, but I'd always considered it was just a matter of degree rather than any real difference. Not so! Indeed, many of them seemed to believe in all sorts of things, often based on personal experience, that most educated people just wouldn't countenance. What I'd thought to be an unusual and medieval way of thinking was actually very common.

I began to suspect that, somewhere along the way, modern medicine had missed a trick or two. However, I was uneasy. I needed to reconcile two opposing worldviews, and I needed to see how, or even whether, it was possible to fit these new skills into my working life as a primary care physician. I'd always been interested in bereavement counseling; I was convinced this new skill could be useful in some cases. On the other hand, there was always the threat of someone not liking what I was doing and making a complaint. And I really didn't need that. I was a successful physician at the height of my professional life with a family to support. Why do this? What a conundrum.

This dilemma occupied my mind and gave me sleepless nights for months. Meanwhile, I was still getting messages coming through while I was seeing patients. For want of making any decision, I decided to just sit back and see what would happen.

On December 6, 2004, a 66-year-old woman entered my room and sat down. Normally bright and bubbly, Lucy burst into tears. I inquired about her background. She'd been born in Ireland but had lived in England for years. Had anything changed recently? No. She'd suddenly been plunged into an extremely deep depression.

"I can't go around like this, Doctor. Can you give me anything?"

Not entirely happy to do so, but feeling I didn't have much else to offer her at that moment, I printed out a prescription for an antidepressant.

I was just about to hand her the prescription when I felt that familiar feeling, almost like a physical slap to the back of my head.

I clearly heard a voice commanding, "Ask her about her father!"

With that, I thought I could vaguely see the outline of a man over her left shoulder. This was utterly unexpected and quite took me by surprise.

I heard myself saying, "Lucy, tell me about your father."

Quick as a flash, she stopped crying, looked at me and said, "He was killed 38 years ago on December 8 by the IRA. Do you think that's why I'm depressed?"

At which point, I described the person I thought I'd seen over her shoulder. It was a good description of her father.

Furthermore, in two days time it would be the anniversary of his death.

Her transformation was sudden, startling, and quite wonderful. She stopped crying, grabbed my arm, and looked at me intently.

"Thank you so much. You don't know what this means to me," she said.

Lucy explained that, although an Irish Catholic, her father had been critical of the IRA. She was living in England at the time her father had been murdered by, she'd always assumed, the IRA. Since then, she'd often felt the protective presence of her father around her. When Lucy mentioned this to her family she'd been told that, as a Catholic, she wasn't supposed to believe in such things.

We discussed how she felt about her father's death and the fact that it was probably its anniversary that had triggered her reaction. I also told her I didn't necessarily subscribe to the survival after death hypothesis.

"Well, you believe what you like, Doctor. All I can tell you is: you've confirmed what I always thought. Now that I know why I was so depressed, I won't need your pills."

She left the room all smiles, while I sat dumbfounded.

One month later she returned.

"What's wrong, Lucy?"

"Nothing at all."

"So why have you come to see me?" I asked.

"I've come to tell you a story." Lucy sat down and rubbed her hands together in excited anticipation of my reaction.

A couple of weeks after our last meeting she'd gone to a party at her Irish social club. A rather creepy man who claimed to have the "second sight" had approached her and said, "Lucy, I've got something to say to you."

"What is it?" she asked.

He motioned her towards a small room off the main function hall.

"It's very personal, so why don't you come into this room?" he suggested.

"I'll do no such thing. If you've got anything to say, just come right out and say it now," said Lucy, doing her best to sound shocked at his impertinence.

"Well, did you know there's a fella looking over your left shoulder? I think he's your father." He then described the same figure I'd seen.

She glared at him and said, curtly, "Of course I knew. My doctor told me that last week!"

Lucy looked at me and smiled.

"You know what, Doctor? That sure took the wind out of *his* sails."

20

Some Subtle Property of Light

It was the beginning of 2005. Punam's father, a retired primary care physician, was then 83 years old. He'd been suffering from slowly progressive Parkinson's disease for some time, but he'd become much more frail since the turn of the year. Just after Easter, he went into hospital with an unexplained fever. He was discharged after a week or so. In April, he was admitted to the Queen's Medical Center in Nottingham. The doctors there discovered he'd developed a liver abscess. His condition rapidly deteriorated and he went into a coma. We rushed up the highway to be with him and spent a weekend hanging around the hospital. It was obvious he was seriously ill, and I pitied the poor young internal medicine resident who had to break the bad news to us. He knew that his patient's daughter, son, and son-in-law were all doctors and much more senior than he was. Furthermore, he also had to face various family friends who were all senior specialists at the hospital. But we all knew what was going to happen. It was just a matter of time.

It was while we were sitting around my father-in-law's hospital bed that I had an unusual thought. It occurred to me that, somewhere else in the hospital, people were gathered around a similar bed, waiting for a baby to be born. I wondered if, somewhere on the Other Side, my father-in-law's deceased relatives were waiting by their equivalent of a hospital bed for him to pass over. As I was considering this, I began to sense the unseen presence of two people, both Indian, including a short woman wearing a white sari. I mentioned this to my mother-in-law.

"That's Daddy's mother and father," she said, in between tears.

Perhaps I was just fantasizing but it was a surprisingly powerful impression.

I had to take the boys back to London for school and left Punam with her mother and brother. I have to confess I'm not the most domesticated male in the world. I'd never used the washing machine in my life. Punam had given me instructions and it seemed simple enough. The machine broke down the first time I used it. The repairman couldn't come for two weeks. When he did come, it wasn't worth repairing.

Personally, I think it expired from the shock of me using it. I managed with laundry detergent and the kitchen sink.

Punam's father was dead within the week. He died on April 14, the day before his wife's birthday. We all thought he'd been trying to hang on for that. Hindu funerals are arranged soon after the death, and there were more than 200 people at the cremation ceremony.

At this time, Joshua was in his high school senior year and applying to medical school. There were interviews to attend, forms to fill out and he also had to take the special aptitude tests required for prospective entrants to medical school. Now he had to cope with the loss of his grandfather as well. We hoped it wouldn't affect his grades. He knew how much his grandfather had wanted him to become a doctor. These were sad and anxious times.

The only real lightness in my life was attending the psychic development and physical circles. With the death of my father-in-law, I realized how serious I was about developing any mediumistic gifts I might have. I desperately wanted to know the reality or otherwise of survival after death.

A part of me was always holding back, though: still critical and quite skeptical about what I was doing. I needed some respectable scientific input into my efforts.

I'd come across the Scientific and Medical Network while attending a study day at a local psychiatric hospital. Dr. Peter Fenwick, a well-known psychiatrist and brain specialist, had given a very interesting lecture on his research into near-death experiences, and he'd mentioned the Network to me. The Network was a group of like-minded scientists and doctors who were interested in the fundamental nature of consciousness and spiritual experiences. I didn't think much about it at the time. I came across the Network again while searching the internet for any scientific research on survival after death. The Network had organized a conference, which was to be held at Lincoln University in August, later that year. The speakers looked interesting. In particular, I noticed one of them was a professor from an American medical school who'd carried out research into psychic mediums. It was billed as "Beyond the Brain VI," so I decided to register for the conference.

The long weekend was like being a teenager back at university, only better because there were no exams. I had a room in one of the student residences on the Lincoln University campus and attended lectures each day. It was a joint conference organized by both the Scientific and Medical Network and the Royal College of Psychiatrists. The speakers reviewed current ideas regarding interesting new research into what makes us conscious, aware beings.

This was wonderful. I found myself among doctors and scientists who were just as interested in this field as I was. Many of them mentioned experiences stranger than mine. I met Doreen, who'd witnessed physical phenomena in séances while on a quest to contact her son who'd died 11 years before. She was convinced a bird had materialized during one séance, and she'd had numerous other confirmations of spirit activity. Sadly, she'd never managed to contact her son.

I also met an anthropologist who'd observed the transfiguration of an African witch doctor during a shamanic ceremony. What he described was very similar to what my sister and I had witnessed with Felicity.

While I felt at home, even here it was obvious I was somewhat unusual because I'd crossed the divide. I seemed to be the only doctor who'd actually decided to go through the whole mediumship training exercise. Because of this I caught the attention of Professor Gary Schwartz.

Schwartz had flown in from the U.S. to present the results of his research into the accuracy of messages given by mediums. Stocky, bearded, and bespectacled, with an entertaining lecturing style and penetrating intelligence, he looked exactly like my idea of a pioneering American academic.

With the title of Professor of Psychology, Medicine, Neurology, Psychiatry, and Surgery at the University of Arizona in Tucson, he seemed well-placed to do research into the accuracy of the messages given by mediums. Much parapsychology research used ordinary individuals who had to try to guess the result of the next throw of dice or next card selected in a sequence. There was a lot of statistical evidence that something other than chance was going on, but the effects were subtle and skeptics were critical of such results.

Professor Schwartz wondered if perhaps this was the wrong approach. He pointed out that if you wanted to see good baseball, you watched the best players in the field. Maybe the same would be true for mediums. To that end, he recruited top American mediums such as John Edward and Suzane Northrop and devised complicated scientific studies to evaluate the accuracy of their messages.

He was convinced there was cast-iron evidence for survival. Furthermore, he said, it would have been even stronger had his deceased mother not kept on trying to get messages to him through the mediums he was studying. While he appreciated her intentions, it tended to spoil the results.

"If you knew my mother, you'd understand this was just like her. She could never keep her nose out of my business!" he joked.

Despite his deceased mother's interference, the results were, in his opinion, still significant. You can read all about his work in his book *The Afterlife Experiments*.

We had dinner together the evening after his lecture.

"I'd really like to explain survival after death without invoking any radical new science," he told me.

"But surely, if we're talking about different worlds then we need some new scientific principle in order to understand this?" I countered.

"Not necessarily." He regarded his plate absent-mindedly, moving his food around with his fork, while he thought about how best to explain himself. Then he looked up at me. "You know, I had this insight while sitting on a balcony one night. It was a clear night and I realized all the light reflected from my body was racing out into space. It's never destroyed. There's also some significant research showing that our body's cells may well use very weak pulses of light to communicate with each other. So, could the key to understanding consciousness lie in some subtle property of light? Maybe consciousness is imprinted on the fabric of the universe in some way via light. Even the terms we use to describe mystical experiences, such as 'illumination' and 'enlightenment,' relate to light."

"Well, you're the professor," I acknowledged. "I'm just an ordinary doctor who stumbled into this, and now I'm trying to understand it in my own way. It's funny. Like most people, I thought mediumship was something you either had or you didn't have; and if you had it, it would be easy. But I'm discovering it's like any other skill; it's probably present to a greater or lesser extent in everybody and, like any other skill, can be improved by training."

"Well," said Professor Schwartz, "that's a matter for debate. I don't think I've ever come across a practicing physician who's decided to explore this field in such a direct manner. Do you know how unusual you are? Why don't you come along to my lab when you're fully developed? I mean it."

At least someone thought I wasn't wasting my time, someone who was academically respectable.

I left Lincoln University on a high.

21

Ghost Hunter

It was one day late in the summer of 2005. I was just finishing off my regular workout in the gym, when I heard someone behind me say, "Ian, you're into paranormal phenomena, aren't you?"

It was Chris, one of my colleagues. Originally from Sri Lanka, he was slightly built with kind, dark eyes. He had trendily shaved his head, and although he was about my age, looked younger. Chris had a family medical practice some distance away in Muswell Hill but lived in Enfield. I rarely saw him, but we'd known each other for years. It seemed word of my unusual interest had spread.

"Why do you ask?"

"I look after Maurice Grosse," explained Chris. "Have you heard of him?"

Of course I had. Maurice had been involved in the Enfield Poltergeist investigation. This had been big in 1977 and had even made headlines in the national press. His co-researcher in the case, the author Guy Lyon Playfair, described what he and Maurice had experienced in his book, *This House is Haunted*, which I'd read many years before.

"Would you like to meet him?" asked Chris.

"I'd love to. Can you arrange it?"

"I know him very well," said Chris. "I'll be seeing him soon. I can mention you to him if you like. If he wants to see you, I'll ask him if I can give you his telephone number."

I was delighted with this. I knew that Maurice Grosse was an authority in his field. He was head of the Spontaneous Cases Committee of the Society for Psychical Research. In other words, he was a ghost hunter, and a very experienced and well-respected one at that. He was particularly interested in poltergeists.

Poltergeists are supposed to be spirits or ghosts that create physical phenomena such as making noises, moving things, or even causing objects to appear out of thin air. They seem to afflict teenage girls especially, often occurring around puberty. While skeptics scoff at such reports, I had no reason to doubt my patient Ray, who claimed he'd witnessed the Enfield Poltergeist.

Ray was a very levelheaded manager of a hardware shop and a diving enthusiast who'd known the affected family. He'd witnessed the levitation of a cup and saucer one day when he was in the house.

"Doc, I couldn't get out of that place fast enough," he confessed.

A couple of days later I received a phone call from Chris.

"Maurice said he'd love to see you. Give him a ring at home." I wrote his number down.

I telephoned Maurice. He seemed pleased to hear from me.

"Let's get together," he said. "I'd find it interesting to speak to someone in the medical profession who doesn't poke fun at this sort of thing, especially as you know the area where it all happened." We arranged to meet at his house in Muswell Hill.

One Thursday afternoon towards the end of September 2005, I parked my car in a quiet street lined with large, late Victorian terraced houses and knocked on Maurice's front door. It was opened by a very short, elderly, balding man sporting an enormous handlebar moustache. There was a quick intelligence behind his bright, pale eyes.

"Dr. Rubenstein?" His handshake was firm and vigorous. "I'm Maurice. Come on in and meet Betty."

He appeared very sprightly for his 86 years and despite his diminutive size, or maybe because of it, his personality seemed larger than life. Here was a man who evidently enjoyed his life and enjoyed the limelight.

He introduced me to his wife who'd been working in the kitchen when I arrived. We went into their large living room where Maurice and I sat down together on comfortable sofas. Betty fussed around us with tea and chocolate cookies, then left to carry on with her baking while we talked.

Maurice told me how he'd become a ghost hunter. Originally he'd been a mechanical engineer and inventor. But his daughter, Janet, had died in a road accident in 1976. He then experienced paranormal phenomena which made him wonder if Janet's consciousness had somehow survived death. His innovative design for rotating advertising billboards had made him enough money to semi-retire in his fifties; Maurice now had the time he needed to pursue his newfound interest in the paranormal.

He approached the Society for Psychical Research and had the good fortune to come across the details of what seemed to be an interesting case in Enfield. It involved two girls and their mother living in a local government authority rented house in Green Street, not far from my clinic. This "interesting case" turned into one of the best and most comprehensively documented poltergeist cases in the world.

Maurice told me what he'd seen. "I had cardboard boxes thrown at me with no visible agency. People say the girls were doing it. There was no way this was possible." His conviction seemed unshakable.

Maurice found the phenomena he was witnessing so fascinating that he lived with the family for a number of months. He observed first-hand the whole range of classic poltergeist phenomena from the movement of objects to fire-setting.

Events took an even weirder turn when one of the girls began talking in an odd-sounding, gruff voice. Electrical sensors showed that she was producing the voice from her throat, but she wasn't using her normal vocal cords to do it. The voice purported to be the spirit of an elderly man who'd lived in the area and whose body was buried in the local graveyard. He gave details about his life and talked about what he'd been doing since he had died. In those days there were no such things as portable video cameras, but Maurice had made audio recordings of the voice and he played them back to me.

For a while, he and his co-researcher didn't know what to make of the information the voice had given them. However, the case eventually came to national attention. Maurice then had the opportunity to play his recordings on radio and TV. Soon after, a man contacted him who claimed he knew whose voice it was: it was his deceased father's. At least, it sounded like his father and all the details of his life were correct.

There was no doubting Maurice's sincerity and intelligence, but it was obvious that the case, while fascinating, had caused him much personal stress. He'd received a lot of criticism from skeptics. I also sensed there might have been some envy from his fellow researchers as he'd managed to scoop such a good case. Maurice was obviously a tough old stick because he'd braved the controversy and gone on to research over a hundred other subsequent poltergeist cases.

"So, what do you think is going on in these poltergeist cases?" I asked him.

Maurice sat back in his chair, his fingers steepled in thought. He paused for a moment, carefully considering his position.

"Some people feel it's all down to spirit influence in these cases; in effect the focus, the person at the center of the disturbance, is a haunted individual. If you like, ghosts haunt places, while poltergeists haunt individuals. Others say it's just down to telekinesis, mind over matter, on the part of the focus, the person around whom these events tend to occur. These people would say that it's all just a manifestation of unexplained mental abilities and would deny the involvement or even the existence of spirits. Of course, other people just blame it all on trickery. Naturally, you have to be aware of this, but in the Enfield case there was enough evidence pointing to something paranormal going on." His sharp gaze softened, as if he was lost in the memories of those events all those years ago.

"And you think..." I prompted.

He sighed and shifted his attention back to me.

"My theory, for what it's worth, is that the focus certainly provides energy. In some cases the focus can even use this energy to affect the environment. At the same time, any passing entity can also pick up this energy and play with it, too. Think of a kid kicking around a football in the park. Then a couple of other kids come around and start playing with it as well. It's like a sort of 'energy football.' Think of the emotional energy children generate when they reach puberty. That's why they're so often the focus of such cases."

This made sense to me and seemed to tie in with what I was learning in my psychic development circle. In order to manifest in the physical world, discarnate entities such as spirits required some form of physical energy supplied by a living person.

"So, in this case the girls provided the energy and a spirit came along and used it to move objects and communicate," I summed up. "That's a very interesting theory."

"If you really are interested in this field maybe you should join the SPR," suggested Maurice. "We need scientifically educated people like you. Mind you, we do get fewer cases nowadays."

"Why's that, Maurice?" I asked.

"Oh, it's the TV and amateur researchers," he explained. "The minute someone thinks they have a case, these people are all over it like a rash. By the time proper researchers get wind of it, the evidence is completely messed up."

He asked me how I'd become interested in this field. I told him about Felicity's face and some of the impressions I'd picked up from my patients. For some reason I felt a bit embarrassed about telling him I'd joined a psychic development circle at a Spiritualist church. Possibly this was because Maurice was obviously Jewish. I realized this because Betty had told me she was baking for the coming festival of Rosh Hashanah. Jews just did not go to church, Spiritualist or otherwise. Maurice was obviously not Orthodox, but from Betty's activity in the kitchen I'd gathered they were at least conventionally observant Jews typical of their generation. I wondered how he squared that with his ghost hunting pursuits.

"I'm not at all religious," I explained, "but I've been surprised at the number of Jewish people who are healers or even mediums, and still seem to be quite happy in their religious practice."

"Of course," said Maurice, "we Jews are enjoined not to dabble with spirits. All I can say is that our rabbi found my work very interesting and once asked me to give a lecture on it at the synagogue."

Another reason for being coy was because Maurice had obviously approached this subject from a very scientific point of view, trying to gather objective evidence. In contrast, I'd thrown caution to the winds and leapt in with both feet. Perhaps he'd feel that, as a man of science, I'd let the side down.

I shouldn't have worried.

"You know what you are, don't you?" he said, after he'd listened to my story.

"No. What?"

"You're an undeveloped medium. I bet the spirit that manifested around your friend Felicity got some energy from you. That's very interesting in a doctor. You should join a development circle."

Funny you should say that, Maurice...

"In fact," I said. "I have to admit I already have."

I told him what I'd been doing for the past year and he seemed to approve.

"I've had a few personal experiences myself, especially after Janet was killed. I never felt compelled to join a circle like you, though. I've always watched from the outside, so to speak. I think it's wonderful you're making the attempt. I think you're very brave. You know, a lot of people will criticize you, though. I've had to put up with a load of old nonsense from various narrow-minded individuals over the years."

We'd spoken for about two hours and it was time for me to leave. We shook hands at the front door. Betty waved at me from the kitchen, her hands floury from baking.

The last thing Maurice said to me was, "You know, there's no doubt at all in my mind that we do survive death."

The next time I heard about Maurice was when I read his obituary the following year. I guess he knows the truth now. I really hope he's been reunited with his daughter.

22

Fellow Traveler

It was now the fall of 2005. Over the summer we'd received some good news: Joshua had been accepted into medical school at Cambridge. He was the first ever student from his school to go to Cambridge. He even managed to get his photo in the local newspaper. Despite our university education, the Cambridge environment was completely alien to Punam and me. When we grew up in the 1960s and '70s, everything was new. I went to a new high school, a new medical school, and I'd lived in a new student residence block.

But Joshua was attracted to the traditions of Cambridge. His college was located in a beautiful and elegant 18th century building. In my experience, most student accommodations were normally fairly basic. However, Cambridge colleges are well-endowed. He had a large lounge, with a bedroom and an en-suite shower-room. They'd even painted his name in neat, flowing script over his door.

We left him and made the short 40-mile journey back home.

I'd spent the past few months sorting out Joshua's computer and printer. I'd thrown myself into this project, while Punam had organized his clothing and food. It was only when I returned home that I realized this had been a ruse, a way of busying myself. I hadn't really prepared myself emotionally for Joshua leaving home. Much to Punam's and Paul's horror, I couldn't stop crying. I was tearful for days. And, as I'd come to expect, whenever I was under emotional stress, odd things started happening again.

I'd known Lynn for some years. I'd looked after her father

during his final illness. Lynn took after her father: like him, she was tall, blue-eyed and fair-haired. She came from a large and somewhat turbulent family. Her father's death had altered the family politics. At the time, Lynn was working as an office manager and had her own apartment. After he died, she gave up her job to move in with and look after her mother. She was very happy with this arrangement. But she was concerned at the changes it had caused in her relationship with other family members. I saw her regularly in my clinic for counseling over a period of two years.

Eventually, Lynn felt comfortable in her new role, and there was no longer any need for us to meet so frequently. But as we approached the end of her period of counseling, I began to suspect I had a similar problem with my own family. In light of the difficulties I was having with my mother and sister, it occurred to me it was worth thinking about why Lynn's mother, Margaret, reminded me of my own. Margaret was a small, intelligent, white-haired woman who trusted me completely and said she always felt better once she'd seen me, even if I hadn't done anything!

"You know what," I confessed to Lynn. "In helping you, I think I've been confronting the problems I have with my own family."

I attempted to apply the insights I'd gained from working with Lynn to my personal situation. Whatever kind of psychological energy had been released in the process, I'm convinced it had somehow catapulted me into the Twilight Zone.

So maybe I shouldn't have been surprised when, one day late in 2005, Lynn came to see me for an appointment.

One of the real joys of my job is establishing relationships with patients that can last for many years. In some cases the bond is particularly strong. I certainly had this with Lynn and so I was surprised she seemed so wary of me. She sidled into my office, refusing to sit down, and kept on glancing at the door nervously, as if making ready for a quick getaway should it be necessary.

"What's up with you, then, Lynn?" I motioned her to sit.

Lynn hesitated by the chair for a few seconds. Then she sat down awkwardly without meeting my gaze. Instead, she looked at her feet and mumbled something indistinct.

"Oh, come on, Lynn," I said. "We've covered so much ground together in the past. I doubt there's anything you can say that will shock me."

She looked up at me.

"I'm not so sure about that," she said.

"Go on, spit it out!"

"You're going to think I'm crazy. Listen, you won't send me away, will you? Don't make me start taking any drugs." Lynn's voice had taken on a pleading tone. She was most definitely frightened, but I had a strong feeling she wasn't crazy. I knew she was psychologically resilient and I'd always been impressed by her mental stability.

"Lynn, believe me, even if you were stark staring bonkers I wouldn't send you away. Mainly because there's nowhere to send you. They sold off all the psychiatric hospitals and turned them into luxury housing estates years ago. It's a good ploy. The lunatics now pay to get in. I might give you a cell phone though; then when you talk to the voices, nobody need ever know."

She relaxed a bit at my jokes.

"Well then, if I'm not crazy you're going to find this story very odd," she stated, looking at me steadily now.

I met her gaze and leaned forward. She knew nothing about what had happened to me since we'd last met; how I'd stumbled into the Twilight Zone and had even established a base camp there.

"Lynn, I bet anything odd that's happened to you, I can outdo. Easily. Let's make a deal: you tell me your story and I'll tell you mine."

She hadn't expected that at all. Lynn settled more comfortably into her chair and began to relate what had been happening to her over the past few months. The story she told me hardly fit any psychiatric condition. It started when Lynn was talking to a close friend, Cheryl, about a mutual acquaintance, Brenda. Lynn mentioned to Cheryl that Brenda had recently had an insect bite. Lynn explained that the bite had become infected and so Brenda had gone to see her doctor to get some antibiotics. Cheryl phoned Brenda to see how she was doing. However, Brenda denied any such thing had happened. Confronting Lynn, Cheryl had asked her why she'd lied to her about this. Lynn was flabbergasted. She was sure it had happened. But, now she came to think about it, she couldn't remember how she'd found out.

Two days later, Brenda phoned Lynn. Just as Lynn had said, she'd now had an insect bite. And it had indeed become infected. And she was now taking antibiotics. Brenda wanted to know how Lynn had known it was going to happen.

Lynn was completely mystified by this and put it down to "just one of those things."

Something similar had happened on two further occasions and warning bells had started ringing in Lynn's mind.

However, what had really freaked her out were the bedroom visitations. On several occasions, she'd woken up to see a man dressed like a Catholic priest standing at the foot of her bed. She assumed she'd become psychotic and was hallucinating. Lynn had become frightened and wanted help but didn't know who to turn to. It had taken her a long time to pluck up the courage to come and see me.

Naturally, I had to make sure she wasn't unwell or under any stress in her life. As I suspected, she had no evident psychiatric or physical condition to explain what might be happening. By this time, I'd had conversations about similar experiences with many of my patients and come to appreciate they were much more common than most doctors realize. Whether or not they represent genuine psychic phenomena is open to interpretation. It's true, however, that many mentally healthy people experience what most psychiatrists would classify as hallucinations.

I was uncertain how to deal with this. First, I reassured her: she was mentally normal and didn't need any medication. From the strictly medical point of view, that was as far as I needed to go. I hesitated and wondered about professional boundaries. Telling Lynn about my strange experiences didn't worry me, but I now felt compelled to cross a line I'd never crossed before. It appeared to me that Lynn and I were on the same path. Somehow, our fates were linked. I'd helped Lynn with her family problems; unwittingly, she'd helped me with mine. I'd then experienced strange events and begun my psychic development; now it seemed Lynn had also started to experience strange events. I knew I had to help her once again.

"Lynn," I said. "I don't think you're insane. I think you need to join a psychic development circle. Why don't you come to mine?"

23

Fledglings

You know you're on the right path in life when things fall neatly into place. I didn't think Lynn would know about Vestry Road Spiritualist Church or where it was, but it turned out she was remarkably familiar with the area. Her sister, Laura, lived not far away, in a turning off Hoe Street in Walthamstow.

"I'll be there this Thursday," she promised.

Lynn took to it like a duck to water. Within a few weeks she was doing what had taken me months to achieve. It seemed she was a natural.

As I had discovered with Keith Hudson, when the student is ready the teacher appears. That certainly also seemed to be the case for Lynn. Soon after she joined the circle, a new member turned up. Kevin Wright was a middle-aged, rather careworn-looking cab driver from Laindon in Essex who worked in the East End of London.

Kevin had come to join our circle on recommendation as his own development circle in Basildon had recently folded. He'd been training as a medium for two years under the tutelage of an elderly and very strict lady. She'd concentrated her teaching on building up powerful visual imagery using meditative imaginary "journeys." Unfortunately, she'd developed a heart condition and stopped teaching. However, she felt Kevin was now good enough to do "rostrum work." This meant she thought he was ready to give demonstrations of clairvoyance to Spiritualist congregations during services. She'd asked Keith Hudson if he would take Kevin on in order to complete his development in the Walthamstow circle.

Many people find it strange that you can train to be a

medium. They think it's something you have to be born with. Kevin's case shows this just isn't true. In fact, he'd never had the slightest interest in anything otherworldly until one of his relatives had died. Seeing the effect it had had on his family, he'd undertaken a course in bereavement counseling and then become interested in the idea of survival after death. Unburdened by any preconceived notions, he'd taken to the training very easily and soon found he was achieving quite remarkable results.

"It was just like watching a film or reading a book," he said to us in circle one day, moving his head from left to right and looking at his palms as he did so, as if he really were reading a book. "People would get into my cab and I could tell them everything about themselves, link in with spirit, give them names, dates, details, everything. It was wonderful. I thought, well, if it's this easy it'll be a cinch. Then one day I opened up and—nothing."

Apparently, this is common to many trainee mediums. At the beginning it seems very easy, then it becomes harder. I found this difficult to understand; after all, in most cases, once you learn a skill it becomes easier with practice. Few people would have the experience of being able to get into the driver's seat of a car for the first time ever, drive the car perfectly, then forget how to do it and have to take driving lessons. This just didn't make any sense to me.

"What happened?" I asked him.

"I asked my guides and they said, 'That's what happens when we do the work for you. But *you* have to learn to do it now and you have to work for it.' And that was when the hard work began."

I had to think about this. I understood that the concept of spirit guides was very important to Spiritualist mediums. And certainly I'd apparently already met two of my guides. But my medical knowledge caused me to be somewhat skeptical about all this. I was still more than half-convinced my so-called spirit guides were really parts of my own mind that had "come out to play." Kevin, on the other hand, was absolutely convinced of the reality of his guides as independent personalities, as were all the Spiritualists I'd met.

Once again, it was my patient Dave Godfrey who explained it to me.

"It's all to do with energy and frequency," he told me when he came for his regular medication review. "You exist at a lower frequency than spirit. In order for spirit communication to work, both sides have to tune in. That means you have to raise your frequency, while those on the Other Side have to lower their frequency. Eventually, hopefully, you meet in the middle."

"So what do guides do?" I asked.

"Well, depending on who you speak to, any number of things. I think the simplest explanation is those on the Other Side are more aware of us than we are of them. There are many spirits who want to get through to us and it's as frustrating for them that they can't as it is for us. We attract like-minded spirits who act as our guides and help us through life. Most people would say they are assigned to us before we are born, but I'm sure others pop in and out as needed. Much of the time they help us without our knowledge, mainly by inspiring us. But once you begin to open up, they have an opportunity to get more directly involved."

"Okay. But what are these guides? Are they really dead people?"

Dave smiled and stroked his luxuriant beard thoughtfully. "Now there's a question. Maybe there are many different forms of intelligence out there. Perhaps it's a case of choose which order of being you're most comfortable working with.

Who knows? Spiritualists believe that most guides are simply the spirits of people who've passed over and want to help those remaining behind."

It sort of made sense, but I was still not sure what specifically a spirit guide did for a medium. At that point, I had supposedly met my guides. I remembered the message from his grandparents I'd given to Dave in the circle. It was one of my most accurate messages so far and I'd certainly asked my guide Kosa for help on that occasion. But most of the time I forgot to speak to my guides and wasn't even aware of their presence. Yet I often still managed to get reasonably accurate messages while sitting in circle. This was all getting very confusing.

It got worse. I'd been doing a lot of reading. It seemed even some very famous mediums weren't sure about their guides, either.

I read about Eileen Garrett, a trance medium in the 1930s. Famous for bringing through the airmen who died in the R-101 airship disaster, she was never convinced her guides, Abdul Latif and Uvani, were personalities totally separate from her at all.

At this stage, I have to confess I was still having a real problem with all these strange ideas. I had developed to the point where I was sure that in order to go further I needed a good practical framework within which to operate. Spiritualism certainly offered that, though its religious aspects didn't appeal to me. However, while Spiritualism's beliefs were intellectually consistent, they seemed just a little too simplistic for my over-complicated mind.

I began to envy those who could just sit back and accept it all without a second thought. Certainly Kevin did and it seemed to have worked for him—but not for me. Every time I tried to contact my guides I began to have tremendous self-doubts and couldn't stop myself worrying about what I was really doing.

I tackled Keith on this issue while we sat in the dark one Tuesday evening, during the physical circle.

"Keith, what do spirit guides actually do?" I asked.

"You mean, what don't they do!" snorted Keith. "Did I ever tell you about the time I was going to go on vacation?"

"No. What happened?" I asked.

"My guide Tsu-Ling told me that as I was having a rest he was going to go off on a vacation of his own without me."

I raised my eyebrows, hitherto unaware they had vacations on the Other Side.

"And..." I prompted him.

"I opened my third eye one day while I was away and there was nothing."

"Nothing? What do you mean?" I asked.

"Just blackness. Oh, it was wonderful! There was nothing to disturb me. I had a good rest. When he came back from his vacation, I could use my third eye again."

Hmm. Just like that. Well. Okay, Keith, I thought, perhaps it was just an unconscious excuse so you could allow yourself to have a rest.

"So, basically, Keith, your guide does what, exactly?"

"Everything. All the gifts. Without him I can't do anything."

"So he does it all for you, then? That means you don't have to do anything yourself, doesn't it?"

"No! He uses my energy. Also, he makes me work for it—he doesn't just give it to me."

This baffled me. If Tsu-Ling did it all, in what way did the medium have to do anything at all?

Keith explained it like this: "Look, it depends on what sort of mediumship you do. If you're a trance medium, they take over completely and do it all. They come in, talk through your body, and do the lot. You just step aside and let them do it. They do use your energy, though. They always need your energy to work on the earth plane."

"Okay, when it comes to trance mediumship, that makes sense," I said. "But you don't do that, do you?"

Keith gave a slight shiver to his voice. "Nah. I don't want any of that. That's not for me. What we do here is mental mediumship. What you have to learn to do is to build up a relationship with your guides so you can work together. It's all about teamwork. You may have lots of guides working with you on the Other Side."

My eyes had become used to the darkness of the room, and I could vaguely see he was using his fingers to count the number of different sorts of guides he recognized.

"I mean, you've got your clairvoyant guides to help you see spirit. Then you've got your clairaudient guides who let you hear spirit. Then you have wonderful philosophy guides like Silver Birch who can give you knowledge. It goes on and on, there's no end to it!"

I had understood that Spiritualists viewed mediums as "instruments," which the contacting spirits in some sense "played" or manipulated in order to bring through messages. This obviously made sense when talking about trance mediumship.

However, Keith's explanation of how mental mediumship worked showed the relationship between guide and instrument could be more complex. The process was also two-way. To some extent, mental mediums could share the abilities of their guides and use them in a kind of reverse process. I'd heard the term "blending" being used. I finally began to understand what it might mean. You could think of the medium as the earthly representative of a team of like-minded individuals, the rest of whom were on the Other Side. Members of the team could share their energy and abilities.

I had to smile. For all the world it sounded like some sort of ethereal medical practice. I would often ask my colleagues for their opinions about problems within their field of expertise and then use their knowledge to help the patient in front of me. Each time I asked for help, I learned a little more and so the next time it became easier. It made a kind of sense.

Meanwhile, it was evident Kevin was on the up. His training had obviously prepared him very well for being a platform medium, and he was ready to demonstrate clairvoyance up on the rostrum during Spiritualist services. He was now officially Keith Hudson's fledgling. A fledgling is a trainee medium who is learning how to give clairvoyance in public demonstrations. Kevin was turning out to be a very good medium. He was a little slow and ponderous at first, but that was only to be expected; it's incredibly daunting to stand up in public and offer to do this kind of thing. As a perfectionist, he was never happy unless his message was absolutely accurate and could be taken by the recipient.

Whatever you may think of Spiritualism as a religion, one thing it does have going for it is its claim to be based on testable evidence as opposed to received wisdom. Of course, its major problem is that most of the evidence, when not downright feeble, is very subjective. But its heart is in the right place: there are no holy books and little doctrine to swallow. It's very freethinking and often attracts people from other religions who like to drop in.

The Spiritualist approach is that the medium should be able to give cast-iron evidence of survival after death. Certainly, Spiritualist services take on the trappings of other religions: the congregation may sing Christian hymns, and there will usually be some attempt at an uplifting sermon (known as an address). But everyone attending a Spiritualist service knows they are there for one main thing: the clairvoyance.

Kevin Wright and Keith Hudson had very different views regarding the sort of messages that should be given during a Spiritualist service.

Keith, who'd been a medium for more than 30 years, would try to give concise messages to most members of the congregation. He was usually very good and he could easily give more than 20 brief but accurate messages in a service. Few members of a congregation left disappointed after Keith had taken a service.

Kevin's approach was different. Initially he'd give the most minute and detailed information to one or two members of a congregation. Gradually, he established a good reputation and began to take bookings for services. Within a very few months, he was his own man, taking services at various Spiritualist churches throughout the north and east London circuit. When he was on form, a congregation could expect seven or eight good quality, though somewhat lengthy, messages seemingly indicative of survival after death.

He still sat in circle with the rest of us but was clearly frustrated with Keith's more easy-going, freewheeling style of teaching. Keith, never one to be hidebound, saw merit in the way Kevin had been taught. He decided to create two circles.

Kevin would take on the more advanced students, those who'd already learned how to open up and were prepared to develop their gifts. This would be with a view to creating platform mediums. Keith would teach the basics to the newer people and those who were just attending out of interest and for the social contact. This would be the larger group. The smaller advanced group would adjourn to the church's library or the snug, while the larger group would use the church's main hall.

Lynn and I were to attend the advanced group. We were now Kevin Wright's fledglings.

24

Hard Work

Almost without my realizing it, what had started as a completely crazy and wild ride through the hinterland of reality had settled down into a much more serious process of personal development.

Although Spiritualism is officially recognized as a religion, it's really more of a movement. It seems to attract a mix of people. They are even sometimes regular worshipers at other churches who are looking for something more. Few of the people attending the development circle considered themselves Spiritualists. Indeed one of the members of the Tuesday physical circle was vigorously anti-religious, having been brought up in a very intolerant Anglican household. He once complained that a particular service had been "too religious." Even Keith Hudson criticized Spiritualists for often being narrow-minded; he considered himself a "Seeker after Truth" rather than a Spiritualist.

Many of the people I met at Vestry Road Spiritualist Church had started attending services after experiencing a bereavement. You could describe others as survivors from the shipwreck of life. These were the ones most likely to be attending a development circle rather than just services. Caught up in strange currents of events, they had waded ashore to the shifting sands of a strange country. Like me, they were desperately trying to make sense of what had happened and where they now found themselves. Despite our completely different backgrounds, we were all convinced there was something going on behind the scenes. However, unlike conspiracy theorists, we thought it was all tremendously uplifting and wonderful—a sort of inverse paranoia.

You can get used to anything. After a while, I managed to put my doubts about what exactly I was doing to one side and just accept where I was. I was helped by Keith's extraordinarily large collection of books on paranormal phenomena that contained some classic works on Spiritualism from its heyday between the two world wars. The stories of how some of the most famous mediums had developed and eventually come to terms with their gifts made fascinating reading.

I still had my misgivings but I needed a framework to give me an intellectual handle on what I was doing. I decided I might as well take what was on offer, albeit with more than a few reservations. This still sat uneasily with my scientific and medical training, and I had a difficult time trying to justify it to my more critical self. Luckily, I knew a little about the history of science and this came to my rescue.

New Age theorists often use the term "quantum" as a catchall to justify their most wacky ideas. Quantum theory, with its idea that tiny subatomic particles can be in two or more places at the same time, does seem very far-fetched. Perhaps one day this will help to explain how psychic phenomena work. But I was more interested in how scientists eventually came to terms with this theory, even though they were much bothered by the implications.

Scientists in the 1920s and '30s decided to use the theory as a kind of model of reality. They accepted it was probably not "true" in any fundamental sense. They thought they would need to change the theory as more evidence became available. It was useful because it helped scientists predict the outcome of certain experiments. In fact, it turns out quantum theory is one of the most accurate theories ever devised. Its ideas are vital in the design of the electronic chips we use every day.

In my own small way, I decided to approach what I was

learning in the same manner as those early scientists. I would just accept what I was learning as a model of reality. It might not turn out to be an accurate account of how things worked, but it did provide a useful framework within which I could operate. Maybe after I'd experienced the whole process, I would understand exactly what was going on.

Then again, maybe I wouldn't. Scientists are still arguing about the fundamental truths behind quantum theory. There's no doubting, though, that quantum theory works—it delivers the goods. I was less certain about mediumship, and even less certain about the validity of spirit guides. But, for the purposes of convenience and dealing with fellow travelers, I was now reasonably comfortable using terms such as the Other Side, subtle energy, chakras, opening up, and grounding.

So, by the beginning of 2006, I felt I'd established a firmer basis for my psychic development. This was handy because I now had to do some hard work in our new mediumship development circle.

We settled into a pattern. Regular attendees included Lynn, Jane, June, Dave, Lindsay, and me. Others came and went as the circumstances of their lives dictated. Sometimes we'd have as many as 10 or 12 hopefuls in the group. Kevin considered that the usual hour starting at 8:00 on a Thursday evening wasn't long enough. He was used to two-hour sessions. We compromised and agreed to try to turn up by about 7:30. People would start filtering into the church once the side door was unlocked at about 7:00.

Most of us were tired and tense from the day's work. We'd take the opportunity to rest and unwind by sitting and chatting until the circles started. Those of us who weren't smokers would have to put up with some pretty serious passive smoke inhalation for a little while. When it was time, Kevin would usher us out of the kitchen into the library or the snug with a call of "Come on, advanced group!" while there would be good-natured catcalls from those remaining behind.

Kevin's teaching method was based on his own experience of learning the ropes. He felt that "going on a journey" should be the bedrock of a medium's development. The purpose of these meditative musings was to improve one's visualization ability and stimulate the imagination.

We're used to thinking of the imagination as something used in the production of fantasy and daydreams. However, the ability to create and manipulate visual imagery is a mental faculty that can be used for more than just fantasy. As far as Kevin was concerned, the only guaranteed way of developing as a medium was to sharpen this faculty and then use it as a tool to receive information.

He approached the business of developing his fledglings in a serious and workmanlike fashion. He felt the quality of his fledglings would reflect the quality of his teaching.

Kevin would begin his sessions by relating the experiences he'd had while giving clairvoyance at various venues the previous week: how the atmosphere had varied at different locations, and how people had differed in their reactions to the messages he'd given. I found this interesting because it revealed the difficulties and surprises a new medium could expect.

Next, he would say a brief prayer for protection, a bit like grace before meals, followed by the process of opening ourselves up psychically.

We'd sit comfortably in our chairs with our eyes closed, feet flat on the floor, and our hands resting uncrossed on our laps, palms down. Kevin would ask us to envisage a light shining beneath our feet. We were to imagine we were pulling this light up our legs to the base of the spine, then up the spine itself until we could visualize it shining out of the top of our heads.

Finally he'd say, "When you're fully opened up, turn your

hands over, palms upwards."

We would then be ready for the guided meditation. Unlike the meditation in Keith's circle, this lasted longer, maybe half an hour or so. Kevin would take us on an imaginary journey, usually starting in the church or at home. He'd ask us to imagine leaving the building, catching a bus or boarding a coach and traveling to an attraction such as a park or a zoo. We also visited medieval banquets, theater shows, fairgrounds, mountains, and numerous other places.

The whole point of this process was to exercise the imagination. He'd often throw in some images such as, "You're passing a group of children riding bikes," and then, after the meditation, ask us to describe the children, the clothes they were wearing, and their bikes. This wasn't easy. Despite his exhortation to "leave your everyday worries outside the door" before opening up, it would often be hard not to experience intrusive thoughts about the day. Another problem I had was sometimes he'd describe something I was able to envisage very clearly. But then he'd spoil it, perhaps by asking us to do something like go along a path I hadn't imagined. I suppose, however good our psychic powers, it would have been too much to expect us all to have exactly the same picture in our heads.

I've always had a powerful visual imagination, but others weren't so lucky and had real difficulty following the journeys at first. On the other hand, my particular problem was getting rid of extraneous thoughts. Each of us, in our own particular way, had difficulties with this process of guided meditation. But the hard work soon began to pay dividends.

"Today we're going to go on a journey to meet our guides," said Kevin one evening. Whatever reservations I had about what guides really were, I had at least established who my guides were supposed to be. While I didn't always sense their presence when working with clairvoyance, I knew how important Spiritualists felt their guides to be.

"If you don't get to know your guides and get a good working relationship with them, you won't get anywhere," stated Kevin, with firm conviction.

He continued. "The first guide you'll meet is your monk..."

Lindsay interrupted. "Excuse me, Kev. What if your guide isn't a monk?"

Kevin looked nonplussed at this. He'd never taught before and found it difficult to stem his flow to answer questions.

He blinked at Lindsay. "What do you mean, 'What if your guide isn't a monk'?"

Lindsay was insistent. "Well, Kev, I know my guide and she isn't a monk."

Kevin leaned forward. "Well, maybe you haven't met 'im yet," he suggested.

Lindsay raised her eyebrows at this. "Are you saying we *all* have a monk?"

"Yes," said Kevin.

Lindsay looked a bit put out. "What about a nun, then? Could I have a nun instead of a monk?"

"Lindsay. What have I just said? We've all got a monk."

She decided to back off. "Oh, all right Kev. I was just asking, that's all."

"Anyway, today you're going to meet 'im."

I couldn't contain myself. I should have known better but I can never keep my mouth shut when I'm fired up about something. Of course, I was excited because, just as Kevin had said, the first guide I'd met had, in fact, been a monk.

"Kev, I've already met my monk. But I have a question. How do I know he's real?" I asked.

Kevin turned to look at me with a very surprised look on

his face. Clearly, his idea of teaching did not involve answering awkward questions from his students.

"What do you mean, 'How do I know he's real'?" he asked.

"I mean, how do I know he's not just my imagination? How do I know I'm not just kidding myself?"

Kevin stared blankly at me for a second or two. His tone of voice took on a slightly dangerous edge.

"Are you saying I'm kidding myself, then?"

He seemed indignant at what he thought was impertinence from his students.

I attempted to explain myself.

"No, I'm not staying that at all. But how do you know these guides aren't just part of your unconscious mind, the bit you've given permission to go off to do the psychic stuff..."

Kevin gave me a reproachful look.

"Ian, I haven't got a clue what you're talking about, mate," he said, settling back in his chair, legs crossed, and arms folded. "We've all got a monk and today you're going to meet 'im." He looked at his watch. "No more discussion! Let's open up and get going or there'll be no time left."

We all met our monks. Even Lindsay.

At the end of the session, as we were clearing the chairs away, it was evident Kevin had taken my questions as criticism.

"Listen, Ian. If you don't believe in your guides, then maybe you shouldn't be doing this."

Lynn intervened at this point. "Kev, I think it must be very hard for people like Ian, who understand psychology and suchlike, to get their heads around this sort of thing."

Kevin thought about that for a while. Then his face cracked into a smile.

"You mean he's a bit too clever for his own good!" he said, laughing.

Lynn had smoothed some ruffled feathers and I realized Kevin, for all his gifts, was not inclined to think outside the box. Never mind, he was certainly worth it. As far as he was concerned, he was devoting his unpaid time to training mediums, not debating philosophy. I decided to save some of my more theoretical questions for Keith Hudson and my patient Dave Godfrey.

Kevin had established the ground rules: if we were in his group, then we did things his way. This was not a debating society. Now that we all understood what he expected, we could crack on. And crack on we did!

25

Don't Feed the Medium

After a few weeks, Kevin explained it was now time for us to try to bring someone in from the Other Side. We were to do this by the simple method of including in our meditation a wooden bench. He asked us to imagine we were sitting on this bench, which might be on a hillside, in a park, or by a river. We were then to imagine someone coming to sit next to us. Kevin wanted us to try to visualize this person very clearly and see what we could learn about them. Then we had to ascertain if they had a message for anyone in the circle.

I relaxed into the meditation and went on the journey. Very soon, I found myself sitting on the required wooden bench. Next to me was a man dressed like a pantomime pirate. I could see him but he didn't say anything. Instead, he held up a bottle of Captain Morgan rum. The next thing I saw was a sort of mental tableau consisting of an old upright piano with a crowd of people standing around it. The man was pointing to the piano, and I got the impression I had to mention it.

After a while, I heard Kevin say, "Now it's time to come back. Say goodbye to your newfound friend."

We mentally retraced our steps. Kevin talked us through to the end of the meditation and we opened our eyes. We all blinked at each other as he turned on the lights, each of us trying to work out who we should give our messages to. I looked at June and guessed mine was for her.

Sure enough, she once knew a man, now deceased, who fit my description. His name was John Morgan. He'd often joked he used to be a pirate and was the original Captain Morgan. When he died, his family had had trouble disposing of his upright piano. He was the only one who could play it and nobody else in the family wanted it. That was a definite hit.

Lynn had also done well, having given Lindsay an extraordinarily accurate message regarding her mother.

Kevin was pleased with our results but told us we had a long way to go.

"You're not working hard enough," he said.

I was working as I'd done in Keith Hudson's circle. I was receiving information but in a rather passive way. The information had been given to me like a parcel. All I had to do was unwrap it and describe what I saw. Kevin explained this was fine when you were starting out.

"But if you do it that way, your guides are doing all the work for you. They've got jobs to do on the Other Side, like bringing in more people, establishing the link, and keeping hangers-on from butting in. After a while, they'll expect you to do your bit. Also, if conditions aren't that great, they may not be able to get as close to you. So you can't just leave it to them."

He described what he was doing when he went up on platform. To help him, he took a card and a pen from his jacket pocket. He wrote something on the card and held it up. We could see he'd written CERT in large capital letters.

"Right then," he said. "I want you to remember this. It reminds us what to do. The 'C' stands for 'communicate.' First, we establish the link and bring the spirit person through. The 'E' stands for 'evidence.' We have to give evidence to the recipient that we have someone with us who they can recognize. Next, we have 'R.' That's the 'reason' the communicator has come through. In other words, that's the message. Finally, 'T' stands for 'tie it all up.' Don't just say, 'that's the message, next one please'—that doesn't come across at all well. Summarize what you've said to the recipient and do it nicely; it just sounds better."

We all nodded in agreement. It seemed quite straightforward and logical. Kevin continued: "Names are often hard to get, so you need to describe the person you can see: tell the recipient how the communicator is dressed; how they did their hair; are they showing you any tools connected with their work? Describe exactly what you see.

"At the same time, you have to constantly be asking them questions in your mind, even while you're describing to the recipient what they look like. Who are you? How did you pass? When did you pass? Are there any names linked with this person you can mention? Are they bringing anyone else with them?

"What you're trying to do is give a picture of this person so the recipient can recognize them. Then, even if you can't get a name, or you get the name wrong, they'll at least know who you're talking about.

"Once you've established who's coming through, you then have to ask why they've come. Is there a specific message? Or are they just popping in to say hello?

"Now, when you've done all that, you then have to break the link. You could just say, 'I've finished,' but it's not very professional and doesn't come across well. Ask the communicator for something special to give the recipient. I usually ask if they'd like to mention any flowers that may mean something to the recipient, or a special object like a piece of jewelry. Also it's good to mention any special dates coming up, like a birthday or anniversary, and then you can say goodbye."

On a good night, a medium on platform may have to give up to 10 of these messages. It seemed like a lot of work.

"You begin to become aware of other spirit people waiting their turn. Your guide's job is to make sure this all happens in an orderly manner. And then you've got your conditions."

Spirit contact is often fraught with difficulties. Although

it becomes routine for experienced mediums, establishing a connection is never an easy task. Conditions such as how the medium is feeling and all sorts of external factors, such as the weather and the atmosphere generated by people around the medium, can all have an effect. Another problem is that in a crowded church hall it's often hard to see which spirit communicator belongs to which recipient. Kevin explained that everything is done by means of "links." Links can best be visualized as lines of energy that establish communication. Like telephone lines, they can sometimes become crossed and messages can go to the wrong recipient.

You also had to be aware of certain types of recipients. Some would be so set on getting in contact with a particular individual, they wouldn't accept anybody else.

"So you get Uncle Bert or someone who comes through from spirit. But the recipient comes expecting their old mum or dad. You do your best with Uncle Bert, but they won't take him. I tell you it can be a real struggle sometimes. You come away thinking you're useless, then next week you see the same person and they say, 'I just realized you had Uncle Bert last week.'" Kevin shook his head. "Meanwhile, you've looked like a right idiot in front of everyone and spent the rest of that week kicking yourself."

Then there were the "message grabbers."

"They'll take any old thing. You give, it they'll take it. It makes it harder because you've then got nothing to give to anyone else."

Finally, Kevin reserved his greatest contempt for those recipients who never, ever took anything. "I honestly don't know why they bother to come! You soon get to know who they are. It's best to steer clear of them. I mean, I had a spirit woman with me the other day. She told me she was this lady's mother. But the lady wouldn't take her. Meanwhile her mate was nodding away and nudging her saying, 'That's your mum!' but she still wouldn't have it!"

So the success or otherwise of this enterprise doesn't just depend on the medium and any communicating spirits. The recipient is equally important. A recipient's cardinal sin, however, is to "feed the medium."

Kevin elaborated on this point.

"What's a medium's job?" he asked, one evening.

"To bring spirits through," said Lindsay.

"Yes, but why do we do this?" he asked.

"To provide evidence of life after death," said Lynn.

"Exactly," said Kevin. "We need to give the evidence. Let's say you're on the platform and you've got Aunt May in spirit with you. She's told you she passed with a heart condition and liked working in her yard and so on. So, you tell the recipient you've got her aunt, but you haven't had a chance to say anything else yet. What do you think happens if the recipient jumps in and says, 'That's my Aunt May. By the way, she had a heart condition and liked gardening'?"

"That's the message gone," said June.

Kevin nodded in agreement. "With recipients like that, you've got no evidence to give them at all. They've told you everything. In fact, they've given *you* the message, not the other way around! It makes it pointless. So just let them say 'yes' or 'no' and nothing else. Okay, sometimes 'maybe' can be useful. But if they try to give you any more information, don't let them. That's *your* job. You can talk to them about the message after the service if that's what they want."

Listening to Kevin reminded me of some of the technical conversations I sometimes had about patients with my medical colleagues. The similarity didn't end there. When I was a medical student, I'd had to learn how to "take a history" from a patient, that is, how to get all the relevant information needed to make a diagnosis. Now it seemed I had to learn to take a history from a spirit person. I just hoped I wouldn't have as many problems learning this as I'd had as a medical student.

"Anyway," said Kevin, as we cleared away the chairs. "Next week you'll have a chance to try this out. I've asked Keith if we can do a fledgling night. Those of you feeling brave enough can go up on the rostrum."

26

Spreading Our Wings

Fledgling night was scheduled for the following Wednesday evening service. Those of us in Kevin's circle who wanted to go up on platform would have the opportunity to test our clairvoyant powers in front of a proper Spiritualist congregation. I decided to give it a go.

That Wednesday evening, I pulled up outside the church, found a parking space, and went to the side door. Momentarily fazed by finding it locked, I realized I was supposed to use the main doors, as this was a proper service. Usually empty, this evening the church hall was packed. Apparently, fledgling services were popular with the congregation, which had been notified at the end of the previous Sunday's service.

Jeff gave me a cheery handshake at the front door.

"Alright, Doc?"

"Yes," I said. "I'm a bit nervous though. Are you going up?"

Jeff shook his head. "Nope. This is just for Kev's students." He gave me a wink. "Go on mate. Show us what you can do."

Keith Hudson was sitting at the back of the hall talking to Jim, the ailing church janitor. Keith gave me a few words of advice. "Just open up and trust your guides. Don't analyze what you want to say, just let it happen. Anyway, I'll be back here seeing how you do, so good luck."

I walked through the hall. Somewhere inside me, a few top gun butterflies had decided to test some novel aerobatic maneuvers. I tried to calm my nerves by thinking of some of the difficult situations I'd coped with in the past. It didn't help. I thought of the lectures I used to give, many years before. That helped a little. But at least then I'd known what I was going to say. This evening I was expected to speak, quite literally, as the spirit moved me—or not.

This situation reminded me of a particular tale I'd heard while sitting in the Tuesday evening physical circle. There was once a medium who used to practice in a very novel manner. Taking the supposition that psychic gifts transcended time and space to its logical conclusion, he would sit down a couple of days before giving clairvoyance and write down the messages he was going to give on little pieces of paper. Up on platform he would choose someone from the congregation, reach into his pocket, draw out whichever scrap of paper came to hand, and then simply read out the message written on it.

"That's how they want me to work," he would explain to a not very enthusiastic audience. Apparently, he didn't get many bookings.

But now I could see he might just have had a point. At least he was prepared.

Not all of us were going up on platform that evening. Some couldn't make it on Wednesdays. Others just couldn't face it. June was one of those who'd decided she wasn't ready. Those of us who were going to give it a go had tried to persuade her to join in. After all, she'd given some pretty good messages in circle recently. What was more, June usually chaired Sunday services most weeks, so she was used to being in front of a congregation. But she wouldn't have it.

"I'm just not ready," she said.

"But you've been sitting in circle for the past nine years, June," said Kevin, pointedly. "If you're not ready now, when will you be?"

June wouldn't budge. "I don't know, Kev. I get stuff but it's just not clear enough. I'm really not ready to go up on platform."

Kevin was waiting for us in the kitchen. Five of us were going up on platform: Lynn, Jane, Lindsay, Dave, and me. With 15 minutes to go before the service started, it was time to open up. We sat in subdued lighting in the church office while Kevin talked us through the opening up procedure.

"Imagine the light beneath your feet. Now draw it up..."

Next, we had to bring in our first spirit communicators, interrogate them, and ask our guides to marshal any other communicators who wanted to come through.

I imagined I could sense the presence of my guide Kosa. I had a clear mental picture of his unshod feet standing on sandy soil with beads around his ankles. But I couldn't tell if there was anyone out there who wanted to come through with a message. Oh, what the hell, I thought. I'd just wing it and see what happened. Even if I got nothing it would still be an interesting experience. I imagined how I'd have reacted if someone had told me, three years before, that one day I would be waiting to go up on platform to give clairvoyance at a Spiritualist church. With that thought, I became more relaxed. There was a soft knock on the door. It was time to go up.

The rostrum or platform (the two terms are used interchangeably) was an elevated wooden dais that ran along the width of one end of the church hall. Few Spiritualist churches are wealthy and consequently it wasn't very grand, but the church members had done their best to spruce it up.

Flowers, real and artificial, stood in vases beneath the platform on a long trestle table, which was covered with a white tablecloth. Next to the vases were a couple of brass candlesticks and a cast bronze figure of hands clasped in prayer. Up on the raised narrow platform was an old upright piano, a compact stereo system, and some chairs. Someone had left a carafe of water and some glasses on a little table for those giving clairvoyance. A small lectern stood in the middle of the platform. On the wall behind the platform was an ornamental plaster rosette, a glass model of an angel in a plaster niche, a large clock, and a framed poster listing the "Seven Principles of Spiritualism." This simple and somewhat haphazard decoration gave the overall impression of dedication to an uncomplicated faith: more chapel than high church.

We climbed the four steps up to the platform in single file. Kevin was already there ahead of us, standing behind the lectern. He chatted to the congregation while we nervously took our seats and poured ourselves glasses of water. He opened the service with a brief prayer and then gave a short address explaining how he'd started teaching and giving his own demonstrations of clairvoyance.

While Kevin was doing this, I found myself anxiously scanning the congregation. There were about 30 people in the hall—quite a good turnout for a mid-week evening.

There are two problems for mediums on platform. Firstly, do they have any decent messages? That much is obvious. Less obvious, however, is what's called "map-reading," that is, if a medium has a message, how do they determine who the message is for? There's no set answer and every medium will have his or her own preferred method. To a large extent, it depends on how a medium operates.

Although the term clairvoyance commonly refers to any information gained psychically, it does have a more specific meaning. Clairvoyance, or "clear seeing," in its strict definition refers to gaining psychic impressions that appear in the form of images. Usually these images are subjective, that is seen with the mind's eye, and very similar to a vivid imagination. Sometimes images can appear to be objective when they appear to be outside in the physical world, just like ordinary objects or people. And sometimes images can appear as a strange combination of the two.

Clairvoyance has its auditory counterpart, clairaudience, or "clear hearing," where the medium gains information in the form of an inner voice. Again, sometimes the voice may be heard as if emanating from the physical world.

Clairsentience, or "clear knowing," is where the medium gains information through intuition. Clairsentient mediums may not see or hear anything but just know what they need to say.

I have a very strong visual imagination, so it didn't surprise me that I mainly received my impressions in visual form. I'd also had episodes of clairaudience and, although infrequent, when they did occur they were pretty spectacular. I'd also learned to trust my intuition. So I guess you could say I can operate using all three.

Usually I just knew who the message was intended for. In circle, it was much more intimate and felt somehow easier. But on that Wednesday evening there were many people I'd never seen before, all sitting looking up at us with expectation. It just didn't feel the same. I wondered how it was going to work for me. Maybe it wouldn't.

I looked at the congregation and waited for inspiration. I had a vague feeling at the back of my mind. It may have been similar to the feeling an angler gets when he feels a fish taking a nibble from his bait. I had something. In fact, I could sense I had a few things. The problem was how to sort them out. I asked my guides for help.

"Come on guys, lend a hand here," I said, mentally.

I imagined a beam of light coming out of my forehead, like the beam from a movie projector. As my gaze swept over the congregation, I tried to visualize the beam projecting holograms of my spirit communicators standing close to their intended recipients. Maybe this would work.

My gaze fell on what was obviously a mother and daughter

pair, four rows back. The mother was in her early forties and sitting next to her, to her left, was her teenage daughter. There was something funny going on over their shoulders. I had the impression of a flurry of activity. This appeared to settle down and stabilize until I imagined I could see the image of a short woman with long white hair standing behind them. She had one hand placed on the daughter's right shoulder. Her other hand was resting on the mother's left shoulder. I could now see this woman clearly, though it wasn't like seeing an ordinary person. It was a case of not quite subjective, but not quite objective, clairvoyance. The woman was smiling at me. I knew all I had to do was mentally reach out and I would be able to find out what she wanted to say.

So far, so good. Now, was there anyone else? I looked around and felt myself drawn to a woman sitting in the right-hand aisle, towards the front of the church. I had the impression of a chubby boy with short hair and red cheeks standing next to her. He looked about 13 or 14 years old. He was wearing a brown fleece jacket, which was zipped up, and he seemed to be trying to shake the woman's shoulder with his left hand. At the same time, he was indicating something with his right hand, which he passed at intervals across the woman's chest. I didn't quite get the same feeling of connection with this image that I'd had with the previous one.

Next, I could see something odd with a woman who sat a few rows further back. I couldn't see any obvious communicators, but I noticed a sort of heat haze rising up from her. It was very clear, so clear that at first I thought there was a heater switched on behind her. The emergency fire exit sign by the door behind her appeared to be rippling in the haze that seemed to go up into the air a good 8-to-10 feet above her head. I didn't know what to make of this but it was quite remarkable.

Now feeling more confident, I had another quick glance

around. The woman and the boy were still at their stations, but now I could also sense a sort of psychic commotion around three people sitting at the back of the hall. It felt as if there was a very excited dog running round and round them, occasionally bounding up and down, trying to get their attention.

I looked at the others. Some of them had their eyes closed, trying to get something. Lynn, sitting to my right, was gazing at the congregation, calmly prepared. She'd obviously made a connection.

Kevin introduced us. "Who'd like to go first, then?" he asked.

We took turns. Lindsay went first, then Lynn. I wish I could remember what their messages were, but I was concentrating so much on my own messages I didn't pay any attention to what they were saying. I was trying to connect with the white-haired lady, but I was forgetting to ask her any questions. Instead, I could just feel bits and pieces of information at the edge of my awareness. Kevin looked at me. I took a sip of water from my glass and stood up.

"I'd like to come to the lady over there," I said, pointing to the older woman. "I take it this is your daughter?" I indicated the teenager sitting next to her and they both nodded.

"Okay. I have an elderly lady and she's standing right behind you." They both gave a sudden sharp look over their shoulders as I continued.

"She's quite petite and has white hair which goes down past her shoulders and she has a fringe. She's got blue eyes." They both nodded.

"I think she's your mother," I said, pointing to the older woman. All at once, I received more information: an image of white sheets hanging on clotheslines, and a bungalow with a neat backyard. I mentioned what I was seeing and once again my recipients nodded and smiled. I mentally asked the

189

woman how she had died and received the impression she'd had a stroke. They could take that, too. Then I had a very clear vision of a silver bracelet. But I couldn't see how it fit in.

"She's just shown me a silver bracelet, or I suppose it could be a bangle. Does that mean anything to you?"

Smiling broadly, the teenager held up what looked like a piece of tissue paper. "Yeah! I just bought this in the market this afternoon." She unfolded the tissue paper to reveal a plain, silver-colored metal bangle.

Her mother said to her, "Gran must have been there and seen you buy it."

Now, this was good. I felt I was getting into my stride. I had the evidence. But what was the message? Ah...there it was. It was for the girl. I just kind of knew what she wanted to say.

"She's telling me you need to pay more attention to your studies. This is your GCSE year and you can do well in your exams if you'd just stop mucking about."

With this message the mother nodded and shot a glance at her daughter who now looked a bit rueful.

I was so carried away I didn't try to get any more information but rather hurriedly said, "Okay. That's all I've got to tell you." I sat down and took another sip of water. I glanced around to look at Lynn but she had her eyes closed and was obviously busy getting someone else through.

My turn again. This time I went for the woman with the chubby boy standing next to her.

"I'm with you," I said. She nodded and looked at her neighbor. They were either friends or relatives. They could have been sisters, as they both looked the same: florid-featured, overweight, and careworn.

I described the boy. The woman folded her arms, grimaced, and shook her head. I experienced a sinking feeling in my stomach. This did not look good. I tried describing the clothes he appeared to be wearing. She still refused to take him. All my confidence evaporated. I didn't know what to do and caught Kevin's eye. He raised his eyes to the ceiling and made a circular motion with an index finger, meaning "wind it up." I muttered an apology and sat down. The two women looked at each other; the woman sitting next to the recipient had a scowl on her face.

My last message had a slightly better reception. I described the "doggy" sensation I'd experienced to the group of people at the back of the hall.

They had a brief conversation and then one of the women said, "We just lost our dog. It could be her."

I left it at that.

After about an hour, it was over. We filed down the platform steps into the kitchen where tea was being served. I was very happy with my first message, but I wanted to know what had gone wrong with the second message. I needed to ask the two women who the boy was.

I maneuvered myself over to them, threading my way through the tea queue.

"I wonder who that lad was," I said to the woman who I thought should have taken the boy.

She gave me a strange, not very friendly look.

"It's her boy," she said, and flicked her head towards her companion. "He died four years ago when he was nine."

Her companion glared at me.

I added up the years: nine plus four. So he'd have been about 13 now. Spiritualists believe that children who die continue to mature on the Other Side. This was all making sense: the boy had been pointing to the woman's companion, not the woman herself. It almost looked as if he'd been trying to shake her to get her attention. I couldn't work out why they were both so unenthusiastic at my attempts to give them a message and I never found out the reason for this. But as far as I was concerned, I hadn't done too badly.

Next, there was the woman with the heat haze. I had to find out what that meant. I hadn't had a chance to mention it while I was up on platform. Anyway, it wasn't really a message at all, more an observation, but it was puzzling me.

I went over to her. She was a pleasant-looking young woman in her early twenties. She seemed pleased to have a chat with me, but when I described what I'd seen above her head it meant little to her.

"Perhaps you saw my aura?" she suggested.

I didn't know about auras. I thought they were supposed to be brightly colored, not like a smoky heat haze.

I needed a coffee. Jeff grabbed my arm and thrust a cup into my hand.

"Well done, Doc. That was great," he said.

I wasn't so sure. I mentioned the spirit boy and how the women hadn't claimed him, even though they'd evidently known who he was.

Jeff leaned forwards to peer around a pillar to get a better look at them. His judgment was simple, straightforward, and cutting. "If you ask me they look like a couple of grumpy cows. Dunno why they bother to come to a Spiritualist church if they don't want to take the message."

Jeff's earthiness made me feel better. He also had an explanation for the heat haze I'd seen. "That was definitely her aura. They're bigger than you thought, aren't they?"

"But I thought auras were like a shining light surrounding the person?"

"Yeah. But when you first start seeing auras they can look just like what you saw or sometimes like smoke." He took a long drag on his cigarette and puffed some smoke up into the air as if to illustrate what he meant. "Anyway, I know that girl.

She's just starting to open up and develop. She's been doing a lot of reading lately. That's why you saw her aura."

Afterwards, Kevin debriefed us in the office. "Well done, everyone. Don't forget to close down. Bring the light back down to your feet."

We sat for a few minutes in silence while we did as we were told. Kevin had noted everyone's messages. Over tea and coffee he gave us his carefully considered opinion regarding our individual performances.

He clearly thought Lynn had given the best messages. Next, he turned his attention to me. "Ian. You definitely got your connections. But you needed to give more detail."

I asked him about the spirit boy I'd seen. What did he think about them not taking my message?

"Well, that's what I mean," he said. "If you'd got a bit more detail from him, then that lady might have taken him." Kevin scratched his chin. "Then again, she probably wouldn't have. She looked like she'd be hard. I'd have probably avoided her."

He didn't think much of my doggy message, but then I suppose it would have been hard to give a message from a dog: "Can anyone take sausages?"

I obviously still had a long way to go, but I felt I'd given a good account of myself. This would have been unthinkable a couple of years before.

Lindsay had done well. She'd managed to give one detailed message that had been well-taken. Like me, her second one hadn't been as good, but at least her recipient had had the decency to take the message. Jane and Dave had picked up something. Their messages hadn't been stunning, but nonetheless had been taken.

The fledglings had spread their wings.

27

Rough Guide

It was a Thursday evening and Kevin was mad. He was angry because his messages had gone flat. He'd had a couple of bookings for churches where he'd had to struggle to get anything at all. His messages had all been taken, but he wasn't satisfied with their quality. Consequently, he was one hell of an angry man.

"I've told 'em. 'If you do that to me again, I'm giving this up,'" I overheard him saying to the others as I came in slightly late to the circle.

"Who's that then, Kev," I asked, innocently.

"My bleedin' guides. They've been 'avin' me on! If they don't buck up I'm giving this up!"

"Maybe you're just tired?" suggested Lindsay.

Kevin sat back in his chair and folded his arms.

"Tiredness don't have nothin' to do with it. I'm going to ask them for a new guide. This just isn't working."

Can you do that? I wondered. Well, why not?

Like Lindsay, I thought Kevin was probably overdoing it. There's no doubt that platform work, indeed any psychic work, seems to be incredibly draining. Kevin was now fully booked, mainly with churches on the East London circuit, and that was in addition to his day job as a cabdriver, plus his teaching work with us. Clearly, he had the potential to become a virtuoso performer and, like all virtuosos, he was a perfectionist, never quite satisfied with his performance.

That evening he was very upset with his guides. A year before, I might have found his anger amusing: a crazy guy raging about *not* being able to hear any voices in his head.

But now I realized just how bad he felt. He had arranged all his bookings, was prepared to stake his reputation on giving decent messages, and now felt his team had deserted him. I didn't envy him.

We spent the session listening to all the grievances he had with his guides.

"Crikey, Lynn! This evening felt more like a Kev Wright support group," I said, as we drove back to Enfield.

Lynn was sitting next to me in the front passenger seat.

"Actually, Ian, I think he's overdoing it. I was there with him, you know."

Kevin had asked Lynn to go and work with him on platform a few weeks before. She'd been very brave but had dried up, stuttered a few messages and, when she'd got home, couldn't stop crying. She'd vowed never to go up again. But Kevin had telephoned her the next day and persuaded her not to give up. He'd taken her out with him on a few occasions when he was working and she was pleased with her progress.

"So, Kev feels he's hit a rough patch, eh? He's a perfectionist though, isn't he? Honestly, how do you think he did?" I asked.

"To tell you the truth, he wasn't bad at all. You wouldn't have noticed if you didn't know him, but I could tell he was struggling," she said.

"And how did you do?"

"Good. Very good, in fact. My Uncle Johnny was there."

"In the congregation?"

"No. He passed years ago. He came and told me he'd be my new guide. He was very helpful."

Lynn gave me a brief resumé of the messages she'd given. I was impressed. I knew Kevin had pegged Lynn as someone to watch, but he'd kept quiet about taking her out as his fledgling. Lynn had come a long way very quickly. I was feeling a bit envious of her progress.

"I wonder if he'd take me out with him as well, sometime," I said.

"He did mention it, as a matter of fact, but he wanted to work on my confidence first. I had such a bad experience that first time. Mind you, the way he's been talking tonight, maybe he'll give up."

"No way!" I said. "Like you said, he's just been overdoing it. He's put in so much effort. I can't see him flouncing away like some prima donna. I bet you he'll be fine next week."

I was right. The next Tuesday evening during the physical circle, Keith Hudson told us Kevin had been assigned a new guide and he was getting on well with him. I wondered who was responsible for making such arrangements.

"Oh, there's a whole organization on the Other Side," explained Keith, as we sat in the snug, the luminous paint on the trumpet and trays glowing eerily in the dark.

He elaborated further: "There's your advanced guides who work out what you need. They can change your normal guides if necessary. Plus they can send you helpers who just drop in for a little while to help out. I mean, we're talking about a whole other world, all organized and arranged."

He had no doubts about this at all. After all, apparently he'd been on trips to the Other Side on more than one occasion.

"My guide Tsu-Ling took me. It's wonderful. They have great halls of learning, huge libraries, theaters, and so on. You'd love it; you can study anything you like!"

Keith waxed lyrical for the rest of the session over the delights awaiting us after we die. It sounded great but, for some reason, I was in no rush...

Just as Keith had said, the following Thursday Kevin was in fine form. Evidently happy with his new guide, he was now in an expansive mood, cracking jokes as he told us what had happened the last time he'd gone up on platform.

We were all relieved.

At the end of the session, he took me to one side.

"Ian, there's no circle next week 'cos I'm working at Ilford. Lynn's coming with me. Do you want to come, too?"

I felt a sudden fluttering sensation in my stomach.

"Okay," I said. "I'll give it a try."

There was no turning back now.

"There's only so much I can teach you in circle, see. You can talk about it all you want, but you have to go out and do the work, or you'll never make any progress. Anyway, it's next Wednesday if you want to come."

"Thanks, Lynn," I said, on the way home. "I assume you told Kevin what I'd said last week."

"I only said that if he asked you to come out with us, you wouldn't say no," she explained.

I was pensive as I drove back to Enfield. I was also feeling slightly nervous about the prospect of going to a strange place and putting myself on the line.

"You know, it's very odd how this is working out," I mused.

"In what way?" she asked.

"Oh, I don't know. You come to see me and I help you with your family problems. Then I find I have similar problems. In trying to solve them, I go all psychic. Then you come in worried you're going crazy, but it turns out you've gone psychic like me. I help you out by bringing you to the circle. Then you streak ahead and help me out by telling Kevin I want to go out on the circuit with you both. Don't you think it's a bit like we're climbing up a rock face together or something? First, one goes up a bit higher and then the other. It's like we're dropping lines to each other as we go. What are the chances of all this just happening randomly?"

I dropped Lynn off at her house and arranged to pick her up the following Wednesday evening.

28

On the Circuit

Things didn't go according to plan. Kevin had double-booked. He'd forgotten he'd accepted a booking to take a service at Hornsey Road Spiritualist Church the same day.

Lynn telephoned me during clinic.

"He said we could do it on our own. What do you think?" she asked.

"Well, they know we're fledglings, what have we got to lose?" I said, trying to sound cool.

"Let's go for it, then," said Lynn. "See you next Wednesday."

Next Wednesday evening was warm and sunny. The service was due to start at 7:30, doors opening at 7:00. I didn't know the route to Ilford very well so I'd left plenty of time to pick up Lynn and take a slow rush hour drive eastwards around London's North Circular Road. The traffic was lighter than I'd expected and we arrived at 6:15. With 45 minutes to kill, we found a pub nearby, sat down at a table, and drank lemonade. We cracked nervous jokes about what would happen if we turned up drunk on strong lager.

We were outside the church at exactly seven o'clock. The doors were locked. Like most of the Spiritualist churches I'd seen, it was a humble, single-story affair.

A woman in her seventies turned up. She wore an impish expression that made her seem younger.

"Hasn't Sam opened the doors yet?" she asked.

"I'm sorry, we're new here. Who's Sam?" asked Lynn.

"Oh. I'm Iris. Sam and Eileen run the place. I thought Sam was meant to be opening the doors. I hope he's got the key."

Iris then told us in exquisite detail about her recent hospital appointment and how she'd been disappointed the doctors hadn't told her anything. I looked at Lynn furtively and she caught my eye. Probably not a good idea to mention I was a doctor...

Lynn changed the subject.

"We're Kevin's fledglings," she said.

Iris thought for a few seconds.

"Kevin. Oh yes, he was at Barkingside a few weeks ago. He's good." She looked at us, mischievously. "Hope you are, too."

A younger woman called Jackie joined us. Then more people turned up. Soon there were six of us waiting outside the church. The doors still hadn't been opened and a debate was going on between the regulars about whose responsibility it was to have the key. It all seemed a bit haphazard and normal, and it took the edge off our nerves. They were just ordinary people. There was nothing to be afraid of.

At 7:45, a well-built, middle-aged man sporting a short beard and ponytail and dressed in casual work clothes walked briskly up to the knot of people now gathered outside the church door.

"Sorry," he said, breathlessly. "I thought I'd asked Eileen to unlock the church, but then I realized I hadn't and I had to go all the way back home to get the key."

He looked at Lynn and me.

"My name's Sam, are you Kevin's fledglings?"

We introduced ourselves and entered the church. It was larger than it looked from the outside but smaller than Vestry Road Spiritualist Church. It had the usual layout: main hall, kitchen at the back, platform at the far end with seats arranged in two aisles. Decoration was minimal.

Sam ushered us into the office through a door to the right-hand side of the platform. The office was simply furnished with a settee, some upright chairs, and a desk with a computer on it. The computer was in pieces, its inner workings trailing over the desk. Sam saw me looking at it.

"Hard drive's not working. Do you know anything about computers?"

"A little. Software more than hardware."

Sam looked disappointed. Possibly he'd hoped I could have done a quick bit of computer repair before demonstrating clairvoyance.

Sam set about transforming himself. His shirt, I noticed, was collarless. It had been unbuttoned when he'd turned up at the door. After he'd done up the buttons, he looked like he was wearing a clerical dog collar. He placed a gold chain around his neck. From the chain hung a green enameled pendant with the letters SNU on it in gold lettering. Finally, he opened what looked like a small broom cupboard and withdrew a smartly-pressed green jacket. Sam had cast off his everyday persona. He was now president of the church and chair of the evening's service.

He rubbed his hands together briskly in a businesslike manner.

"You can both do clairvoyance, I take it?" he asked.

We nodded.

"Good. If you get stuck, I'll link in with you and help out. So, all we need to decide is what else we should each do. I'll do the closing prayer. One of you can do the opening prayer. I suppose that ought to be the person who isn't doing the address." He looked at us quizzically. "Who's doing the address?"

I looked at Lynn. Lynn looked at me. We both looked at Sam.

"Actually, Sam, we've never done opening prayers or closing prayers or addresses. We just do clairvoyance," I said.

"Yeah," put in Lynn. "And we're not that good at clairvoyance, either."

Momentarily, Sam looked fazed.

"I see," he said, sighing a little. Sam ran his hand across his beard, choosing his words carefully. "Look, I don't know how you're being trained. But I have to say this is an SNU church, and the SNU has a set order of service. If you're going to give clairvoyance at a service, then you have to know what to do and what the order of service is."

It occurred to me then that Sam was a religious man. Here was the first truly religious Spiritualist I had met. Fair enough. I was on his turf and he had a perfect right to expect things to be done his way. Besides, I had very quickly warmed to him. He radiated a genuine friendliness and good humor, which made him immediately likable.

"Okay, never mind. I'll do the address and prayers this time. Maybe next time you could try?"

This was good. He'd more or less offered us the opportunity to come again, sometime.

"We have fledgling nights three times a year," he explained. "It's very important to get new people prepared to do the work."

Sam asked us how we'd started training and we each told him our stories. Sam had become interested in Spiritualism by a similar set of curious circumstances. He worked as a hospital chef but in his spare time was a member of the Sealed Knot, the English Civil War enactment society. He first realized he had unusual gifts when, during an enactment weekend, someone had fallen into a patch of nettles. He'd watched while one of the other members, who claimed to be a healer, had run his hand over the inflamed skin and the rash had simply faded. The healer had told Sam he could do this as well. Sure enough, when he tried, Sam found he also had healing powers.

He discovered he could train as a healer at his local Spiritualist church. He joined the church and found the atmosphere very convival. Soon he was on the church committee and attending local Spiritualists' National Union branch meetings. Eventually, he began to develop mediumistic abilities and strange things had started happening to him.

He told us about the time he woke up to go to work and got into the hospital kitchen, only to find he was on the wrong shift. Instead of it being nine o'clock in the morning, it was actually 3 a.m. Somehow, he'd driven in the dark, past several public clocks, without realizing the time. He'd sat in the hospital kitchen feeling confused and wondering if there was something wrong with him. Then he'd become aware of a spirit presence in the room, at which point he felt compelled to give a message to the duty chef, whom he knew only vaguely, about the man's father. At that moment, the duty chef's cell phone had rung. His father had unexpectedly died a few hours previously.

"I couldn't have them getting me out of bed at three in the morning, could I? So I decided to get it under control. I teach mediumship and healing now."

It was a good story and he'd managed to relax us both. He left us for a while to open up and then we went up onto the platform.

There were about a dozen or so people in the congregation that evening. We gave two messages each. They were nothing spectacular but good enough. The intended recipients could understand the messages and we hadn't looked like fools. I learned a lesson, though. I'd wanted to give a message to a woman at the back of the hall. The problem I had was I couldn't tell who I was receiving the message from. Every time I glanced in her direction, I received a vivid impression of an old shed which had an equally old spade propped up against it. The shed appeared to be surrounded by a rather ramshackle garden plot.

This impression would then be replaced by the mental image of a string of very large onions. The only other impression I gleaned was a strong sense of peace and satisfaction associated with these images.

I held onto the message until the service was over. Finally I plucked up the courage and spoke to the woman about this. She was in her seventies, slender, and somewhat timid. I described what I'd seen.

"Oh, bless you. Thank you," she said. "My husband had a vegetable garden like that. That old spade was his and he was proudest of his onions. They won prizes you know!" Her eyes were sparkling and she gave me a kiss on the cheek. Hmm. Why hadn't I had the confidence to give her that message when I was up on the platform? I resolved that next time I wouldn't hang on to any messages.

Sam debriefed us over coffee in his office. "You did well. You've obviously had some good training." He gave us the date of the next fledgling evening. "You're both very welcome to come again."

I did come the next time, but Lynn couldn't make it because Kevin had decided to take her out with him elsewhere. It was now fall when I stood up on the platform to give my address.

I'd taken what Sam had said last time to heart. I'd made up an opening prayer, a closing prayer, and written an address: a brief sermon.

Traditionally, addresses in a Spiritualist church are given without notes. Like Quakers, Spiritualists are meant to talk as the spirit moves them. However, as I was new to this, Sam allowed me to use notes. He'd explained over the phone that an address is supposed to illustrate one or more of the seven principles of Spiritualism. I'd chosen principle five: personal responsibility.

I gave the address but had pitched it more at the level of a medical audience rather than that of a typical Ilford resident. Sam understood it but I'm not sure anyone else did. My clairvoyance was better.

As I gazed out over the congregation, I turned on my imaginary projection beam. Gradually, I became aware of spirit figures appearing in the room.

At the back of the room was a spirit gentleman who looked like my old Uncle Sam. My Uncle Sam always wore a black homburg hat and an old, faded dark overcoat. This "Uncle Sam" was standing behind a woman in her early sixties, with smartly coiffed white hair. The woman was sitting in a chair next to the aisle. To her left, sitting in a wheelchair placed in the aisle, was a young disabled woman whose head was twisted uncomfortably to one side.

"Uncle Sam" was holding something in the crook of his left arm. As I looked, I could make out what appeared to be three long loaves of bread. I felt this man had probably lived in a rural area, somewhere quite rustic: possibly rural France.

"I'm with you, I think," I said to the smart woman.

"God bless!" she said. This seemed to be the standard acknowledgement given by Spiritualists when picked for a message by a platform medium. She had an Irish accent and looked at me expectantly.

I described what I saw. Then I had a flash of inspiration and said, "This gentleman reminds me of my Uncle Sam. Well, obviously it isn't my Uncle Sam but I wonder if he might be your uncle?"

The woman nodded and said, "I can take that."

There was no message from him.

"I'm not getting anything else from him, I'm afraid," I confessed.

"No, I wouldn't expect you to. I'll explain later," she called out.

Something caught my attention along the next row in front. I thought I could see a golden-haired little boy wearing Victorian clothes. He was sitting in the aisle, cross-legged on the floor. He radiated a quiet calmness but I couldn't pick up anything else. As he'd appeared beside a dark-haired woman who was sitting in the aisle seat, I assumed he belonged to her.

I pointed to the dark-haired woman and described what I could see.

"I'm sorry," she said. "I don't know who he is."

By now I was certain he was there. I made a more determined effort to focus my attention. The boy seemed to be wearing a sailor suit. She still couldn't take him.

I'd been concentrating so hard on giving this message, I hadn't noticed that the Irish woman sitting behind her had put her hand up in the air. Feeling a bit lost at what to do next I glanced at Sam who pointed to the Irish woman.

"Can you take this, Maria?" he said.

"I most certainly can," she said. She looked at me and asked, "Can you get a name for this little lad?"

"Er... I'll try," I said. Something popped into my mind. I dismissed it and concentrated, hard. Nothing. Whoops, almost missed it! I grabbed for the thought I'd dismissed. Simon. No. That couldn't be right. What the hell. "Simon," I said.

"Oh, I thought so! I've really got to tell you this! Do you mind, Sam?" asked Maria.

"Go ahead," he said.

"This little boy isn't for that lady." She pointed to the dark-haired woman. Then she addressed me. "You thought it was for her because he's sitting next to her. But who's he sitting in front of?"

Now that Maria had brought it to my attention, I noticed he was sitting on the floor in the aisle in front of the young woman in the wheelchair, literally at her feet.

"I suppose he could be with the young lady in the wheelchair," I said, hesitantly.

"Yes," said Maria. "This is my daughter, and when she was very young, she often used to say she could see a little boy. She said his name was Simon and he looked like the boy you've just described. I'm a medium but I couldn't see him and I really thought he was just her imaginary friend. I always wondered about him, though. But you got him, sailor suit and all."

Sam cut in at this point. "Okay, Ian. Let's see what we can do with this. See what you can find out about this boy. What do you think he's doing here?"

This was turning into a teaching session. And by now it was evident to me who the boy was.

"I think he's her spirit guide," I said.

Sam nodded and smiled. "Yes. It's a bit obvious, isn't it? What I mean is this: why do you think he's her guide? What is he trying to do? Ask him."

I looked at the boy. I mentally asked him the question. He didn't speak, but as I asked him what he was doing for the woman in the wheelchair, I felt the aura of calmness he was radiating become stronger.

"He has to keep her calm. It's very important for her to keep calm," I said. Maria nodded at that, as did a few of the other members of the congregation who obviously knew her daughter.

Sam pressed me. "Why, do you think? Why does she have to keep calm?"

I had a vivid impression of thunder and lightning. I knew immediately.

"She suffers from epilepsy and gets fits when she gets upset." I'd finally nailed it. Sure enough, she was a cerebral palsy sufferer and had severe epilepsy.

"Well done," said Sam. "Do you have any other messages?"

There was one more. To my right, at the front of the congregation, I received an impression of someone who would have driven a large, red car. I sensed a rather tough-minded man and had fleeting visions of a used car lot, which I felt was somewhere in Romford.

I thought it was for a couple sitting in the front row. They could take it. A relative had recently died who fit my description. There was a message this time, a warning to be careful of a business proposition. They could take that, too.

Sam gave the closing prayer and the service was over.

Maria, the Irish medium, approached me just as I was about to step down from the platform,

"Listen," she said. "That was very good indeed. The man you saw was my uncle. You gave a good description of him. He lived in the country in Ireland, not France. He used to wear the clothes you described and his job was to drive a bread delivery van. It was very rural where he lived. He was a very quiet man, never said more than two words to anyone, so I'm not surprised he didn't have a message. In fact, I'd have been surprised if he'd had one. And as for Simon, well, I'm over the moon with that one. Like I said, I'm a medium and I do platform work. If you ever want to come out with me as my fledgling, just let me know."

It was time to retire to the kitchen for tea and some very appealing chunky chocolate cookies. I was ravenous and very tired.

"That's the energy you used up," explained Sam. "You'll need to replace it. You'll be exhausted tomorrow."

The next morning, I yawned my way through my clinic but felt better after my lunchtime swim. It was Thursday and I decided that, despite my tiredness, I ought to go to the circle that evening.

Lynn and I compared notes. Lynn had gone out with Kevin

the night before and done extremely well—indeed Kevin had felt she'd given better messages than he had.

We were elated. On the way home, we discussed the little trip-ups and difficulties we'd experienced and how we'd worked around them.

We also had another venue to look forward to. Kevin had told us there was a fledgling night scheduled at Oxford House in Bethnal Green in late November—six weeks' time. We were definitely up for it.

29

A Measure of Control

Fall and winter are busy seasons for primary care physicians. People get sick as children go back to school after the summer break, meet new viruses, and then bring them back home. So, on top of all the routine illness management, there are also the minor, and not so minor, infectious illnesses to sort out. I also do a lot of counseling, especially bereavement counseling. Now I found I could add a few psychical insights into these consultations.

It wasn't uncommon to have a few messages from the Other Side come through. I'd learned to tiptoe around any information I might have gained psychically until I was sure my patients wouldn't be upset by anything I might say. Invariably, if I decided to give one of my patients a message, it would be very helpful. Often, consultations would then go off in interesting, creative, and surprisingly therapeutic directions.

However, this all took time, and time, for a doctor, is a very precious commodity.

Keith Hudson was adamant.

"You shouldn't be doing it at the clinic, Ian," he said. "You'll wear yourself out. Then your platform work will suffer. I mean, it's different energies, isn't it? You're either working with healing energy from spirit, or you're bringing messages through and using your own energy. If you're healing, you shouldn't be giving messages. You see, as a doctor, your healing guides will be working with you, even if you aren't aware of them. And giving messages will just interfere with their healing."

Kevin was equally skeptical about combining the two. "If

anyone comes through while you're with a patient I'd tell 'em to sling their 'ooks. You'll wear yourself out. Get your guides to keep 'em away. How would you feel if any of their living relatives started knocking on your door when you were with a patient? You wouldn't stand for it, would you?"

I must admit, he had a good point there. Just because someone was dead, it didn't give them the right to start butting in and interfering!

Whatever the technical and ethical reasons for being more reticent, I'd noticed something else about messages given one-to-one—they tended to make me a bit lazy. I'd receive an image that might mean something to a patient. They'd elaborate on it. I'd then receive something else that would allow them to elaborate further.

I discovered I could use my brief messages as a way of developing the consultation, with the patient doing most of the talking. This seemed to help people gain some insight into the nature of their problem. Often the discussion would become very deep and we'd explore what they thought their purpose in life was. I called this process Intuitive Exploration, and I was sure it could be of great use in dealing with some of the problems I saw everyday as a doctor. However, it wasn't the same as being on platform. Regardless of its therapeutic benefits, from the viewpoint of a working medium, it was sloppy. I just didn't have to work hard enough.

"If you stop giving messages in your clinic, your messages in circle and on platform will get better," Kevin reiterated, after a circle where I'd given some very lackluster messages.

I had to think long and hard about this. It used to be said the job of a doctor was to amuse patients while they got better on their own. To a great extent this is still true today, a fact which modern medicine ignores at its peril. Even if, ultimately, giving messages from the Other Side was just an exercise in self-deception, the psychic element had certainly spiced up my consultations. But there were obvious professional dangers, besides the fact that, whatever I was doing, it was very tiring. I had to get a grip and curb my enthusiasm.

Keith suggested I should have a word with my guides. "The trouble is, like attracts like. You tend to attract guides who are like yourself. They're probably as enthusiastic as you are. It's a case of teamwork. You all have to learn how to work together. Tell them!"

I decided to give it a go. One evening, I made an effort to sit quietly, open myself up, and have a good chat with my guides. Of course, I may very well have been talking to myself.

Anyway, the conversation, or monologue, went something like this: "Right then, you lot. I know you mean well, but this can't go on. Let's agree you'll keep anyone who wants to come through off the premises until I open up properly. Let's maintain a channel though: I'll trust you to bring someone through if you think it's absolutely vital. Okay?"

Could I detect a murmur of agreement? I wasn't sure.

Just to be safe, I decided to do a bit of work on myself, as well. I imagined my enthusiasm as a very energetic puppy dog. I spent some time really trying to visualize the dog: he was a friendly, bouncy thing. He was the sort of dog that immediately greeted you when you rang the front door bell: paws-crawling-up-your-legs friendly, tongue-lollingly friendly. I imagined slipping a lead onto his collar and gradually reining him in. Finally, he was sitting by my side, calmly. I mentally threw him a treat. I think he deserved it.

Whatever I'd done must have worked because consultations suddenly became very ordinary. I missed the thrill of seeing if I'd tuned into something or someone but, sure enough, I felt less tired and my messages in circle began to get better.

"At last!" said Keith, when I told him. "That's what your

guides *should* be doing—protecting you. You don't want any old Tom, Dick, or Harry knocking on your door whenever they fancy."

I'd finally managed to achieve a measure of control. It had been a long time coming. I felt less drained and more— what was the word?—grounded. Ah, yes! I'd truly come to understand what "grounded," that most overused and misunderstood word in the psychic vocabulary, actually meant.

As Keith had said, "If you're going to have your head in the clouds, then you need your feet firmly on the ground."

30

One Winter's Night

It was ten o'clock on a Wednesday night in November 2006. The phone rang and I could hear Punam talking.

"Ian, it's Louise, she's got a problem." Punam handed me the phone.

Louise was one of our closest friends. She was a nurse and health visitor by training and had been vice-chair of a well-known charity and interest group. Louise was head of child protection for Enfield and was never usually one to panic. However, now she sounded agitated.

"Ian, can you come around to Hilary's house tonight? She thinks she's got a poltergeist! It attacked her son!"

At any other time, I would have been keen to go. However, I was deep into the process of relaxing, trying to psych myself up for my fledgling appearance at Oxford House in Bethnal Green the following evening. Uncharacteristically, this had involved a rather large single malt whiskey.

"Well, sure I'll come," I said, uncertainly. "But I can't drive, I've had a drink."

"Oh, don't worry about that," said Louise, breathlessly. "I'll pick you up in 10 minutes."

Punam looked at me, one eyebrow raised quizzically. She can do that.

"Louise's friend Hilary says she's got a poltergeist," I explained. "Louise is picking me up in a few minutes."

I knew Punam wouldn't object. If Louise said she needed help, we both knew she really needed it. Louise was usually the one offering help, not asking for it.

"A poltergeist? Are you going to be all right? What can

you do?" asked Punam.

"I haven't got a clue," I confessed. "She seems very agitated."

We discussed how I might handle the situation. Poltergeist or not, Louise was clearly upset, and I guessed Hilary and her son would be even worse. As a physician, I was used to seeing people in all sorts of anxious states. I would reserve judgment and treat it as a standard house call, diagnosis uncertain for the time being. If the diagnosis turned out to be poltergeist, as opposed to hysteria, I could always phone Keith Hudson. And if it was indeed hysteria, well, that would be bread and butter medicine, which I could handle on my own.

Louise explained to me what had happened as we drove the short distance to Hilary's house.

Zachary, Hilary's 13-year-old son, had been in his bedroom putting away some clothes. After a few minutes, his parents had heard screams coming from their bedroom and had found him standing in a corner of the room in a dreadful state. The only person they could think of to call was Louise because of her expertise in child welfare. Zachary was terrified of remaining in the house and so Hilary had taken him across the road to Margaret, her mother, who lived in the house opposite. Zachary was now refusing to go back home.

Louise parked her car outside Margaret's house and rang her doorbell. Although I'd met Hilary before, I'd never met her mother. I wasn't sure how I'd be received.

Margaret opened the door. She was a pleasant-looking woman with short brown hair, aged about sixty. She appeared calm but was obviously bemused by the whole affair. Behind her, looking pale was Hilary. Behind Hilary, looking even paler, and visibly shaking, was Zachary.

Louise introduced me. "This is Ian, he's a doctor," she said. Zachary backed away, clearly not liking the idea of seeing a doctor. Louise noticed this and added, "Zach, although he's a doctor, he's also an expert on ghosts and spirits and wants to hear what happened to you."

Still wary of me, I eventually managed to coax the story out of Zachary.

Zachary had been in his bedroom putting some socks into a drawer. Because it was dark outside and his curtains were open, he could see, reflected in the window, the upstairs hall through the open bedroom door behind him.

He thought he'd seen someone go into his parents' bedroom and had a strange feeling it wasn't a family member. At the same time, he heard the clattering of horses' hooves, which seemed to come from behind the house. Going into his parents' bedroom to investigate, he noticed the bed was rocking backwards and forwards with no visible human agency. He tried to stop it by sitting on the bed, but it got worse and he began to feel something trying to grab him, seemingly from beneath the bedclothes. At this point, he started screaming.

It sounded like something out of a horror movie—the product of an overactive imagination. I thought it unlikely that any paranormal phenomena were involved. It was now late, I had my fledgling night the following evening, and I'd somehow become involved in a late night house call for people who weren't even my patients. Thanks a lot, Louise!

But Hilary and Zachary were convinced something supernatural had occurred. Zachary had never acted like this before, and there was something else as well: Hilary clearly remembered starting to experience supernatural phenomena when she was Zachary's age. For some years, as a teenager, she often used to wake up in the middle of the night, aware of the spectral form of a man standing at the foot of her bed. Sometimes this man would even tuck her in. In addition, she and her mother had often heard footsteps on the stairs when there was no one there. Hilary still occasionally received psychic impressions, and she wondered if Zachary was starting to "open up" as she had done at his age.

Whatever had happened, clearly the family was very upset. I managed to convince Zachary to show me his room. We walked the short distance to the house, Zachary holding his mother's hand for dear life. I tried to think of a strategy that would be helpful for the family. If I were to express my skepticism bluntly, I knew I wouldn't carry them with me. I would have to validate their experience in some way but, as a doctor, I would also have to be honest. This was going to be tricky.

Hilary's house was a mid-terraced Victorian property, larger inside than one would have suspected. Zachary's bedroom was upstairs at the back of the house. We trooped into his room. Louise and Hilary looked at me expectantly

"Can you sense anything, Ian?" asked Louise, intently.

I closed my eyes and attempted to reach out with whatever psychic powers I could muster. There was absolutely no sense of anything unusual at all.

"Can't pick up anything," I said. I looked at Zachary and winked. "You must've scared it away." Zachary didn't look too pleased at this. I had to think on my feet.

"Okay," I said. "I'm really not sure what happened here, but I think we can all agree Zachary has opened himself up to something. Now it may just be an attack of the heebie-jeebies or maybe you're just more psychic than I am. Either way, I need to close you down."

Zachary and Hilary both nodded. Good. I was being sufficiently vague.

"Zach," I said, "as well as a doctor, I'm also training to be a medium. In order to contact the spirit world you have to be 'open,' like a radio that's turned on. Sometimes, however, you can open up without meaning to. Are you feeling upset or worried about something? I've noticed I tend to open up sometimes if I get upset."

"Yes," said Hilary. "He's had some trouble at school recently."

Aha! We'd struck gold. We talked about this for a while and pretty soon I found I'd managed to win Zachary's confidence.

"Okay, Zach. I'm going to teach you a simple technique for closing yourself down and grounding yourself. It will make you feel calmer. I want you to practice this every day."

I took him through the grounding procedure Eleanor the Channeler had taught me. Hilary and Louise went through it with me, too. Within a few minutes everyone was much calmer. After we finished we went into Hilary's bedroom.

The scene couldn't have been more peaceful. Zachary's two younger brothers were lying across the bed, snoozing quietly.

"I think that's the last we'll see of that." I stated, firmly. Zachary and Hilary were looking relieved. It was my first "exorcism"—or maybe not...

Louise looked at Hilary and nodded. "I told you he'd know what to do," she said.

It was now 10:50 and I was mindful of my looming fledgling night. I was convinced this evening had been merely a distraction. Certainly nothing supernatural had occurred.

Zachary went to bed. The rest of us made our way back to Margaret's house.

"Ian, thanks for helping me out with Zach," said Hilary. "You know I mentioned that man I used to see at the foot of my bed?"

"Yes," I said.

"Would you mind seeing what you can pick up at Mum's house before you go?"

I was reluctant. I was tired and I really wanted to get some rest. But something made me say, "Yes, of course," which is how we all ended up sitting in Margaret's dining room at eleven o'clock at night, me with my eyes closed asking for psychic inspiration with three women solemnly waiting for me to make a pronouncement.

Very sensibly, Margaret's husband would have nothing to do with it. He was watching a soccer match on TV. He had cheerily, and possibly dismissively, waved to me as Margaret had closed the sitting room door to keep out the noise. "He doesn't believe in any of this," she whispered.

I was sitting opposite Hilary at Margaret's large pine dining table. The two older women were sitting on a small settee against one wall.

Okay, I thought. Let's do this properly. I opened myself up psychically and asked my guides to come through. I was vaguely aware of Kosa. Now, what could I possibly sense?

I began to feel that I was sitting in an older version of the house. We were in the dining room, but now it seemed to me as if it had somehow become an old-fashioned kitchen. The decor was dark and Victorian. Sitting opposite me was a man. He looked about 40 years old with neatly combed hair. He was wearing a pinstripe collarless shirt and suspenders, the casual clothes of a Victorian clerk or working man. I described him to the others.

"That's the man who used to stand at the foot of my bed!" exclaimed Hilary.

I received an unspoken acknowledgment from the man. Then I had a conversation with him. It was somewhat one-sided. I would ask him questions using my inner voice. I would receive answers clairsentiently, not so much by hearing them, more as a form of knowing.

He let me know he used to keep an eye on Hilary when she was younger. She reminded him of his own daughter when she was little and he liked to make sure she was safe and well. Next, he showed me animal cages. I thought they were birdcages, but I couldn't be certain.

"Monkeys," said Margaret.

"Monkeys?"

"Yes, there were monkey graves in the yard. We found them when we first moved in. They were very old."

Monkey graves. Spooky. I didn't know what to make of that. The man gave me no information about monkeys. Instead, he was showing me coal. There was coal everywhere, great shiny lumps of it. The word anthracite came into my mind. He was showing me lumps of anthracite.

This meant nothing to Margaret or Hilary. The man then showed me the railway, which was nearby. I gained the impression he either worked on the railway or possibly used the railway to get to work. I mentioned this but, of course, this wasn't information we could confirm or refute.

"See if you can get a name," suggested Margaret.

I did so. Martin. Definitely Martin, though...I couldn't say how I knew it.

"He's giving me the name Martin," I said. "Do you know any Martins?"

Hilary looked puzzled. "I have a friend named Martin," she said, hopefully.

"No," I said, shaking my head. I was somehow receiving more information. "I think Martin's *his* name. He's telling me he was the original owner of the house."

Margaret stood up. "Oh, that's easy to prove one way or the other," she said. "I've got all the original papers upstairs. I'll go and get them."

We waited in silence while Margaret went upstairs and brought down a large folder containing a sheaf of papers. She opened the folder and spread the papers across her and Louise's laps. She found the document she wanted. The title deed was a large piece of paper, yellow with age, handwritten in flowing Victorian copperplate script.

Margaret and Louise scanned it for a name. Finally, Margaret stabbed an index finger at the bottom of the page.

"There. Oh my God! Martin! It really is!" she said.

Louise looked and gave a little yelp. "Ian! It really is Martin, look!"

"You must be joking!" I said.

Margaret held the title deed up, triumphantly. It was signed Richard Martin. He'd been the original owner.

So you really are there, I thought.

Quick as a flash I heard Mr. Martin say, in my head, "Of course, I am. Why? Did you doubt my word?"

I was now able to hold a proper, albeit internal, conversation with this Mr. Martin.

"Of course, in my day the backyard was much bigger. It's shrunk a bit now," he said. How do yards shrink? I wondered.

"He's telling me the backyard's shrunk somehow," I said.

Margaret nodded and explained. "The bottom half of the lot was sold off before we bought the house. They were going to build on it but never got around to it. The woman who owns it lets me use it for gardening, but it doesn't actually belong to the house anymore."

Next, he was telling me about there being wells and springs on the site. Once again, Margaret confirmed the details.

Then he told me he had to go. Before he went, he wanted to let me know someone else wanted to speak to me. Then he was gone. And, just like that, the strange sensation of sitting in the Victorian kitchen was gone.

I looked at Margaret. Someone was standing behind her. I knew it wasn't a physical person. There was the vague outline of a short woman.

"Margaret," I said. "I've got someone here for you, I think. Do you know anyone named Hilda?"

Margaret shook her head.

"Are you sure?" I asked Margaret. "She's showing me a bunch of flowers, I think they're lupins. Oh, and there's something about her leg. I can't quite make it out, but for some reason her leg and the lupins are linked."

Margaret looked mystified. Louise was crying.

"Ooh, Ian. You've got my mum."

Louise's mother had died just a few months before. I'd thought the woman was with Margaret.

"Louise," I said. "It could just be from my unconscious mind. I mean, I did know about Hilda."

"Yes. But you didn't know about the lupins," she said, drying her eyes.

"What's so special about lupins?"

"She was very fond of them. When she was a little girl, she once picked some to give to her older sister, my Auntie Madge. She climbed over a fence to get them and cut her leg very badly. It took ages to heal and she always had a small scar there. Whenever anyone asked her how she got the scar, she always mentioned the lupins."

That got me thinking. I knew I'd never heard that story before.

And then she was gone, too. I'd run out of juice. I felt completely drained. It was now past midnight and definitely time for bed.

As Margaret and Hilary showed us to the door, I received one final impression. I looked at Margaret and heard myself asking, "Have you got gypsy blood in your family?"

"As a matter of fact, I have, on my father's side. My grandfather," said Margaret.

I shrugged. "Maybe that explains it. I get the impression

you're psychic as well as Hilary."
    I still don't know where that came from.
    I was tired. Punam was in bed when I got back home.
    "How did it go?" she asked.
    "You'll never believe what happened..."

31

East Enders

Oxford House is in Bethnal Green in London's East End and looks like an old Victorian school building. But it was built in the 1880s to house the 19th century equivalent of a community development project. It's still in use as a community center today. Every Thursday, the members of the Spiritualist congregation known as the "Spirit of Holiness" meet there for a service, followed by tea and a chat.

That evening, Kevin Wright was giving clairvoyance and Lynn and I were accompanying him as his fledglings. We were both looking forward to the evening. Lynn had been going up on platform with Kevin for a number of months and she'd become very confident in her messages and presentation. Although I'd had much less experience than Lynn on platform, after my performance at Margaret's house the night before, I too felt very confident.

We arrived early and found our way to the meeting room that had been booked for the service. Kevin hadn't turned up yet and the organizers were arranging chairs in rows and setting up a large table at the front of the room. The table had been covered with a white paper tablecloth. On it stood some vases of flowers, a large pair of silver candlesticks holding lighted candles, and a carafe of water with glasses for the mediums.

As people filtered in through the door there were a few faces that looked familiar. Iris, the lady we'd met at Ilford Spiritualist Church, was there and also an elderly couple I thought I recognized. They may have been in the congregation at Ilford but I couldn't be certain. However, the gathering was mostly made up of people I'd never seen before, and this evening it looked like it was going to be a full house.

As soon as Kevin arrived, he ushered us out of a side door into a narrow, dark corridor.

"Right," he said. "It's a bit cramped but it'll have to do. We can open up here."

Someone brought out three chairs for us and we sat along the wall going through the process of clearing our minds, drawing up the light from beneath our feet, and asking our guides to come in with any spirit communicators.

The first person who came into my mind was a youngish woman dressed in late Victorian costume wearing a high-necked blouse and full skirt. I had the impression she used to teach at Oxford House and seemed to approve of how the chairs in the meeting room had been arranged. It seemed to remind her of her old classroom. As she had no message, I politely asked her to step aside.

My next image was very cryptic. I saw a huge chain. Its links were enormous and the chain appeared to wind around a very large capstan. As I followed the chain with my inner eye, I could see it rising up into the fore of the hull of a large ship. It was a mooring chain. As I realized this, I could see a tall, thin, jaundiced-looking man standing by the chain. He told me his name was Jim and that his message was for "the big fella in the other room." That was all I got.

Soon it was time to go back into the meeting room. I looked at Lynn. "Have you got anyone?"

"Yeah. How about you?"

I nodded. "I think so, but he's not giving me much."

The room was now full with maybe 40 people or so. We were introduced and Kevin gave the opening prayer and a short address, chiefly consisting of telling the congregation about Lynn and me.

I knew Kevin would expect us to start giving messages very

soon. I scanned the congregation looking for "the big fella." He was unmistakable. Large in every way, even sitting down he towered above the others. He was sitting next to a slightly less large woman who was dripping with cheap jewelry. I guessed she was his sister, as they looked so similar. The pair of them appeared to be in their forties.

Lynn kicked off with the first message.

"I'd like to go to the lady over there." She pointed to the woman sitting next to the big fella. They glanced at each other after the woman acknowledged Lynn. They were obviously together. Lynn had made contact with someone named James who claimed to be a relative. James was showing Lynn brass ornaments and various decorative features relating to a house from the woman's childhood. Lynn described what he was showing her. The pair, who were indeed brother and sister, nodded at Lynn's description. It was apparently an accurate account of their old family home. Neither could place the name James. I had a sinking feeling. Obviously, if they couldn't take James, they were hardly going to take the name Jim!

Lynn had finished and Kevin looked at me. "Anything, Ian?" he asked.

I stood up.

"Yes." I pointed to the big fella. "I have a gentleman with me. He's looking very yellow and skinny." By now, I had a clearer image of what he looked like. He was showing me how he'd looked before he died. "He's showing me a lump in his left groin. I think he died of cancer. I'm sorry but he's giving me the name Jim."

The brother and sister looked at each other, startled. Obviously the penny had dropped.

"That's Uncle Jim!" said the big fella. He had a Scottish accent. I glanced at Lynn who raised her eyebrows. It just went to show how sometimes recipients weren't able to take messages which were clearly meant for them. I suppose they'd always thought of him as Jim, not James.

Having established the link, I now received a flood of information. I saw myself, as Jim, sitting with my legs dangling over the side of a dock, eating sandwiches from a lunch pail. The dock was huge and I had the impression it wasn't in the UK. I described what I saw.

"He worked in the docks in New York," said the big fella.

Next, I was shown what looked like a compost bin. I passed it on.

"He grew prize roses. Always said it was down to his compost," explained the big fella's sister.

Okay, Jim, I thought. What's the message? I didn't hear it, but I knew what I had to say. "He's telling me you've been keeping something secret for some time now. You weren't sure what to do with it. He's saying it's now time to bring it out into the open."

I had no idea what the secret was. I asked, mentally, but got a definite feeling of, "that's not for you to know, just tell him."

I relayed this message to the big fella. He sat back in his chair, now looking very relaxed, beefy arms folded across his chest, with his legs stretched out in front of him like a man vindicated.

"That's just what I needed to hear," he said. "God bless!"

Kevin gave a message and then it was Lynn's turn again. Meanwhile, I was trying to see if I had any more messages to give. I let my gaze sweep over the congregation. I couldn't see anything but I kept on being drawn to the elderly couple I thought I'd recognized. They were sitting in the second row, just to my right.

They appeared to be in their late seventies. He looked vigorous and was very smartly-dressed, wearing a tweed jacket with a shirt and tie; she looked rather frail and was wearing a green woolly coat. It took me a while to realize I was being drawn back to them, but eventually I became aware of a sort of tugging feeling at the back of my mind. Very gradually, I could see an image building up in my mind. It was of a man, possibly in his fifties. He had very curly, dark hair. He was wearing a leather vest studded with all different sorts of badges. I couldn't get his name, but he was pointing to what appeared to be a patio composed of block paving. As I looked, I could see that three of the blocks were set too high. With that, I could see the elderly woman tripping over the blocks and falling. The message was clear. It was a warning.

I gave the message to the couple. The man was very succinct.

"Yes," when I mentioned the dark-haired man; "No," when I mentioned the badges; "Yes," when I mentioned the patio; "Yes," again when I mentioned the blocks being too high. Finally, he said, "Well, I don't know about the badges, but that's my old friend Tom. We just had a patio laid in block paving and three blocks need leveling off."

"I think Tom is telling you to get it fixed before your wife takes a tumble," I said.

He nodded in agreement. "I'd better do that, hadn't I?"

I was doing well. Anything else? I reached out. By now, it felt effortless. It just seemed to flow.

I scanned the congregation again. Right in front of me were a couple of women. Both were well-dressed, much better turned out than the other women in the room. They looked similar. The younger one appeared to be in her early sixties and had shoulder-length blonde hair, almost certainly dyed. The older lady had a perm and looked to be in her eighties. Mother and daughter? Possibly.

"Ian, do you want to go again?" asked Kevin.

I stood up and looked at the two women in the front row. I knew I had to give them a message. It almost seemed as if my Uncle Barney were sitting next to them. Obviously it wasn't my Uncle Barney because he had no business being there. But it looked like Uncle Barney: bald, short, wearing outsized clothes, and with his trousers drawn up almost to his chest. He was sitting in a large red leather Chesterfield armchair. He was waving what looked like a sheaf of tickets, which he held in his left hand. They looked like either airline or theater tickets. I went for theater tickets.

What was the message?

"Tell her 'thank you for looking after me' and not to worry about the business. It's in good hands."

I described what I could see and what the man had said. They took it all. It was the younger woman's cousin. During his last illness he'd had no one to look after him. He'd moved in with her and she'd cared for him for the last six months of his life. The message was reassuring: she'd just agreed to pass on her design and print business to her son but was worried he wouldn't cope. And what about the tickets?

"Last year I won three theater tickets in a competition," explained the younger woman. "The tickets expire at the end of next month. I was looking at them just before I came here, wondering when I was going to be able to use them."

The service finished on a high. Everyone was impressed and Kevin felt we'd done him proud.

"It's all down to good teaching," he quipped. He left pretty quickly; it was a fair old journey to his house in Laindon from Bethnal Green and he had to be back in his taxicab office in Bethnal Green first thing the following morning.

There were two mysteries I had to clear up before I left. Firstly, I wondered why the spirit called Tom had shown me a leather vest studded with badges. I asked the elderly gentleman about this.

"Tom was a close friend of mine from way back," he explained. "I knew him for years. We were at school together. He died about 15 years ago from a heart attack. I honestly can't think why he showed you a leather vest with badges." He thought for a moment and then said, "But you know, now I come to think of it, when we were at school he had a badge collection, loads of them. So maybe that's what he meant?" Perhaps, but he still couldn't place the vest.

Next, I was determined to find out about the big Scottish fella's secret. What was he supposed to reveal?

He told me while we drank coffee out of disposable plastic cups.

Contrary to his appearance, the big fella was actually a trained electronics engineer whose expertise was in cell phone technology. He'd designed a system to help improve the usability of cell phones. He'd had the idea six years before but the technology hadn't been up to it then. However, advances in electronic chip design had made him reconsider trying to interest a company in his system. He'd been laid off only the week before and was considering writing to one particular company with a proposal. In fact, he'd come that night with the hope of getting some indication as to how to proceed.

Lynn shook her head in disbelief. "You know what? To look at him you'd think he was a bouncer or something. It's funny how we both got the same man. I suppose Jim wanted to make absolutely sure his message got through."

We drove back to Enfield, pleased with our progress. We'd both done well; much better than we'd thought we could. But it had been tiring and we felt drained.

"Lynn, where do you think this is taking us?" I mused.

"Goodness knows, Ian," she said. "I'm just going to go with the flow I suppose."

"I'm still wondering how this fits into my medical career," I said.

"I can see how that might be a problem," she acknowledged. "Maybe you ought to just trust spirit?" she said, as I dropped her off at her house.

32

Under the Sign of Cancer

The following evening I received a phone call from Louise.

"Hi, Ian, I just thought I'd let you know that Hilary's done some research about her and her mum's house."

"What did she find out?"

"A couple of interesting things, actually. Firstly, the coal you mentioned—apparently there was a coal yard next door to the house when it was first built."

"So perhaps that explains why he was showing me anthracite. What else did she find out?"

"This has to do with the sound of horses' hooves Zach heard. Hilary found an old map in the library archives. There used to be stables just behind her house. Maybe Zach had tuned into this."

I'd heard of the idea of information from bygone days being imprinted on the fabric of buildings in some manner, like a recording. It had been suggested that some psychically gifted individuals could possibly have the ability to "replay" such recordings, which might account for some ghost sightings.

"Okay. Thanks for the feedback."

"Oh. One more thing, Ian. Ola and David are going to arrange a get-together one evening. There's someone they'd like you to meet."

"That sounds very mysterious. Who is it?"

"His name's Charles. He must be in his eighties: very interesting, highly educated, speaks about a million languages. I've met him and his wife, Rita, a couple of times. He's one of Ola's Polish friends. Apparently he's into Spiritualism and Ola told him you were, too. He said he'd like to meet you. Anyway,

Ola will try to arrange something, either this side of Christmas or in the New Year."

Ola was a Polish urological surgeon who'd come to England to be with David, her English husband. She'd eventually gone into family practice and worked with Mike, Louise's husband. She had links with the expatriate Polish Jewish community, which is how she'd met Charles.

I'd met Ola on a few occasions over the years, mainly at medical meetings. She'd grown up in Communist Poland and declared herself a rationalist but found my paranormal stories fascinating.

"Okay. That sounds like it would be an interesting evening," I said. "Maybe Ola will give us a call then?"

I was in the gym a few days later when Catherine approached me. She pulled back her long blonde hair from her neck, tilted her chin up, and pointed to the right side of her throat.

"Ian, what do you think this lump is?"

This threw me as I wasn't in medical mode. I gathered my thoughts and felt the right side of her neck, at the front, under her jawbone. I could feel a firm lump.

"It's a lymph gland. How long have you had it?" I asked.

"Oh, perhaps a couple of weeks or maybe a bit longer. Possibly a month. I think it's getting bigger. I'm not really sure. It doesn't hurt." She looked worried.

"Have you had a sore throat recently?" I asked.

"No, I'm never ill. Anyway, I've booked to see my physician tomorrow. I just wondered what you thought."

"It's probably worthwhile going to see your doctor. It might be a good idea to get it looked at by someone at the hospital."

"Do you think it's serious?"

"Not likely to be," I said. "Especially as you've only had it for a short time. But it's probably best to get it checked out."

I met her again a few days later.

"My physician's referred me to hospital. He says I should get an appointment in a couple of weeks."

Her specialist saw her in his clinic and arranged to do a biopsy. He took a small core of tissue from the lump using a special hollow needle. Catherine received the biopsy result about three weeks before Christmas. It was cancer, but they couldn't tell where it was from. There were hints it could have come from her pancreas. She would need to have the gland removed, hopefully before Christmas.

This was serious. Life-threateningly serious. If it was pancreatic cancer and it had spread to the glands in her neck, then there was probably little hope for her. Catherine had a reputation for being a fabulously fit fifty-something who looked after herself. She dressed well, looked great, and trained like an athlete. However, over the past few weeks her training had become erratic and it was now becoming evident she'd started to lose weight.

She had the gland removed and was discharged from the hospital on Christmas Eve 2006. She and her husband, Ted, had the most miserable Christmas imaginable. In the New Year, she was transferred to the Royal Marsden Hospital for further tests. She kept me informed of her progress. Her doctors still couldn't find out where the tumor had come from, but they didn't think it was from her pancreas. Good news at last! She would now need a thorough exploration of her throat and nose.

At the same time, my cousin Frances developed a recurrence of her breast cancer. Her original tumor had been diagnosed in 2002, and, following a mastectomy, radiotherapy, and chemotherapy, she'd done well. Eventually, Frances resumed her busy life as a school principal and was looking forward to her retirement in about six months' time. Recently she'd developed a chesty cough, so she'd gone to see her physician. He'd diagnosed asthma, but the inhalers he'd given her didn't seem to help.

Then Frances received a letter summoning her for jury duty. She didn't think she could sit in court for very long because of her cough and came to see me for advice about deferring her jury service.

Punam noticed her right upper eyelid was drooping. "What's wrong with your eye, Fran?"

"I was going to ask you about that. My eyelid's gone all droopy."

I took a look at her eye. The eyelid was half-closed and the pupil was constricted. She had Horner's syndrome. I experienced a sinking feeling in the pit of my stomach. Horner's syndrome in a woman with a previous history of breast cancer and a persistent cough could mean only one thing—the cancer had spread and she'd developed secondary tumors in her chest. Her breast cancer was now at an advanced stage.

I was able to arrange for her to see her cancer specialist very quickly. Her specialist broke the news. She would require more chemotherapy. Frances was devastated.

Life as a primary care physician always involves dealing with people's tragedies and you develop ways of coping with it. But to have a friend and a close relative suddenly become seriously ill in very similar ways was troubling.

Catherine's specialist discovered she had cancer of the back of her tongue. She wouldn't require surgery but she would need a lengthy course of radiotherapy. It would make her feel very ill. Luckily, she wouldn't lose her hair.

Frances was not so lucky. Her specialist had started her on chemotherapy immediately and she'd already lost her hair.

It was now February 2006. I was in the gym talking to

Barbara. Barbara was one of my patients and I'd known her for years. She worked as a beautician, but was also a trained astrologer and a gifted psychic. She'd always assumed I was skeptical about her psychic gifts and was pleasantly surprised when I confessed I seemed to be developing a few of my own. We frequently met in the gym and, as she was also very friendly with Catherine, we three would often train together. Because of her illness, Catherine hadn't trained for months, and Barbara and I were sweating it out on the exercise bikes together.

"Ian, I'm very concerned about Cathy."

"So am I. But there's not much we can do except wait and keep our fingers crossed. She's having the best care in the world."

Barbara gave me a knowing look and said, in a conspiratorial tone, "I'll have a word with them." She pointed upwards. Barbara had a thing about angels.

"Okay. Why not? It can't do any harm," I said, not very enthusiastically.

Barbara punched me playfully on the arm.

"You'll see," she said. "You just need to believe in it a bit more. How can you doubt so much with all the things you've experienced?"

I sighed, deeply. "When you've seen as much illness as I have, it can all get a bit depressing. Also, it's been a bit quiet on the psychic front."

"How do you mean?"

"I can't sense my guides. I feel sort of flat, like I can't get a connection. My messages are absolutely crap at the moment," I said.

"Well, it's not surprising. I mean, your job's hard at the best of times, now you've got Cathy and your cousin on your mind. Your energy levels must be low."

"Yes." I pedaled faster. "I know all that. I keep on telling myself the same thing. The trouble is, when you're used to just reaching out and, well, touching something, knowing it's there, it feels pretty awful when it's not there. Do you ever get like that?"

"Of course. We all get like that now and again. Mind you, I've never really sensed any guides, even at the best of times. I just ask my angels for help. I'll get them to send you some white light."

I groaned inwardly. I was still not quite certain about spirit guides. And when it came to angels... The minute anyone mentioned angels I felt as if my mind were sinking into a fluffy mess. I wouldn't let my head fill up with what I considered to be the mental equivalent of pink cotton candy.

Despite being psychic, Barbara clearly had not been reading my mind because she was still talking.

"Getting back to Cathy, Shirley knows people. Maybe she'll come up with something. You remember Shirley, don't you?"

I nodded. Shirley was her friend and mentor, an astrologer whom I'd seen in my clinic as a favor to Barbara. Shirley had insisted on repaying me by casting my horoscope. This had been a few years before I'd become interested in psychic matters. Interestingly, she'd told me that by the time I was in my early fifties I would have developed psychic gifts of my own. Shirley was into angels, too.

"Well, it can't do any harm, can it?" I said, then, "Ow!"

Barbara had punched me again. This time harder.

Maybe she really had read my mind.

33

A Little Bird Told Me

I tried to meditate. I'd got out of the habit of doing it over the previous year. I lay across the settee in the attic. Although it was a cold winter's day, the sunlight through the attic window was warm.

I needed to talk to my guides. There was a place I used, a mental image. I needed to go there.

I imagined a golden thread of light coming down from the ceiling. Before it reached me, it opened up into a beautiful dome of purple light, shot through with gold rays. The dome surrounded me and, as it did so, I visualized a thread of green light coming up from the floor beneath me. I allowed the green thread to expand into a bowl of green light, surrounding both me and the descending dome of purple light, like green sepals at the base of a flower enclosing its folded petals.

I now had a clear visual impression of being in the center of a double sphere of light. The innermost sphere was purple and represented my link to the spirit world. The outermost sphere was green and represented my link to earth and my protection.

I visualized the inner sphere filling up with a pure white light as energy poured into it through the golden thread above and the green thread below. I basked in the light for a while and then concentrated on trying to picture the double sphere rising up the golden thread, higher and higher.

Eventually it stopped rising and I visualized the top part of the sphere opening up fully. I was now in what I called my observatory. Above me, I could imagine the infinite reaches of the universe. I was standing on a smooth, jet-black surface. In this place, I could meet my guides.

I imagined walking towards the meeting place. Usually I could picture my guides waiting for me, but this meditation wasn't turning out as I'd expected. There was no one there. My mind began to wander and I had trouble holding onto the image. It was useless. I lost whatever connection I'd had and found myself back in the real world.

As I got up off the settee, I had a thought. "If you can't come to us, we'll come to you."

I hoped the thought was from my guides.

It was a Saturday morning and we'd invited Frances for dinner that evening. I was looking forward to seeing her, but I wasn't looking forward to the inevitable discussion. She'd finished her chemotherapy and it hadn't really helped.

I was doing some shopping and had just popped into the local bookshop. I had a quick glance at the science fiction section. I immediately had a very odd train of thought. It's very hard to put this into words, but I'm going to try because it illustrates how some people would say spirit works when it needs to.

I happened to notice a couple of books by a science fiction author named Allen Steele. I had a soft spot for Allen Steele.

Firstly, he had, more or less, the same name as my Uncle Alan, whose surname had also been Steele. Like my father, Uncle Alan had been a London cab driver. When I was young, I'd spent a lot of time in his company playing with his daughters, my cousins Deborah and Susan. When I was 12 years old he developed a malignant brain tumor and had to have surgery to have it removed. What struck me most as a child was that after his brain operation he wore a dark woolly beanie because his scalp had been shaved. He'd always been a quiet and somewhat reserved man. I remember being shocked at seeing him swearing like a trooper one day after his operation. He was attempting to paper his bathroom ceiling and was having difficulties. I guess the operation or the tumor had affected his coordination and he was feeling frustrated. After about eight months his condition deteriorated and he died.

Another reason for having a soft spot for the author Allen Steele was because he'd written a very good book called *Lunar Descent*. This called to mind another science fiction book I'd enjoyed. I suppose it was because the title was similar. The book was called *The Descent of Anansi*.

I happened to be reading *The Descent of Anansi* while I was applying for jobs in family practice. Steven Barnes was one of its authors and the book contained a character named De Silva. A friend of mine had suggested I apply for a job at a primary care practice I knew only vaguely. I wasn't certain about applying because it wasn't situated in an area I knew particularly well. However, the names of the doctors caught my eye: Drs. Barnes and De Silva, the very names in the book I'd been reading. I decided to apply. I'm still there.

My train of thought had somehow connected the author Allen Steele with a book he hadn't written but which had the name "Anansi" in the title.

Musing over these thoughts, my gaze ran along the bookshelves. I didn't fancy either of the Allen Steele books. As I looked along the row of books, I noticed there was a book with the name "Anansi" in the title. I looked again. This book wasn't *The Descent of Anansi* but *Anansi Boys*, a fantasy novel by the author Neil Gaiman. I'd never read anything by Neil Gaiman and, being a bit conservative in my reading habits, walked away.

Then I stopped. Hang on. I recognized that feeling. Was someone trying to get me to buy the book, *Anansi Boys*? By now, I knew how these things were supposed to work. Was my deceased Uncle Alan trying to get me to read the book? Crazy? Yes. True? Possibly. I bought the book and took it home.

I read it very quickly. The story begins with a woman dying of breast cancer in the hospital. She doesn't know it but her estranged husband is the spider god, Anansi, in human form. He makes her better for a brief period. The story continues with Anansi's son going off on a quest. The bird goddess, Anansi's rival, tries to thwart this quest by sending huge flocks of birds to attack him.

This rang a bell. Long before he fell ill, I remembered Uncle Alan joking with my father, saying he'd come back as a little bird when he died. And the reference to breast cancer was also startling. I felt like a detective on a trail.

Over the dinner table that evening, I asked Frances if she remembered Uncle Alan.

"Of course," she said. "He was a kind, wonderful, intelligent man. I loved him."

I'd had no idea she'd been so close to him.

The next day was Sunday. I telephoned Uncle Alan's daughters and told them what I'd experienced.

Susan was at a conference. "Strange you mentioning this. I was just sending an email to a friend and mentioned Dad, which I don't often do." She was interested and open to the possibility of her late father being around but...well, there was nothing evidential.

Deborah was as skeptical as ever and hooted with laughter. Never mind.

It was now Monday morning and I was about to start my 8 a.m. clinic. All thoughts of spirit contact were banished by the grim necessity of getting my first cup of tea while my computer booted up. I went into the back office behind the reception desk to say hello to the receptionists.

"Hey, Ian, did you send one of your spirits to me last

night?" asked Marie, looking up from her filing.

Marie was a good-looking, fashionably dressed Mauritian of about my age. Her job was to chase errant test results from the local hospital. She was also a devout Christian who found my experiences deliciously spooky, not least because she admitted to having had a few psychic experiences herself.

"What do you mean, Marie?" I asked.

"Oh, I had the strangest dream of my life. It felt so real I just wondered if it was anything to do with you. I dreamed I was here in the receptionists' office, at my desk sitting next to Carol. The window was open and a little bird flew in. It landed on top of my head and started tapping me with its beak. Then it flew over to Carol and then flew back onto my head. It started tapping on my head again, like it was trying to tell me something. Then I woke up and thought it must be for you. Now, what on earth can that mean?"

Of course, I knew immediately what it meant.

"Hmm. I think it was my Uncle Alan, and I think he's been trying to get my attention."

I remembered the thought I'd had after my failed attempt at meditation. Was it possible that, as I couldn't get through to my guides, they were doing their best to get through to me? Maybe they couldn't do it directly because of my lack of energy? Had they chosen Marie because, being psychic, she was receptive to their influence? I told her the story and it gave her the shivers. Personally, I think she likes having the shivers.

That evening, I received a phone call from Deborah, Uncle Alan's older daughter. She thought I might be interested in what had happened to her. Her husband, Malcolm, had ordered a folding bike the week before. She only found out the make he'd decided to buy when he came home from work that evening. Deborah, though still skeptical, felt compelled to phone me.

"This is probably really stupid but I had to tell you. He's gone and ordered a German bike made by a firm called Riese and Muller."

"Okay," I said, wondering where this was going.

"Well, it's the name of the model of the bike that really caught my attention, after what you'd said on the phone. It's called a Birdy."

In the 1980s American TV series, *The A Team*, the lead character, John "Hannibal" Smith played by George Peppard, had a catchphrase, "I just love it when a plan comes together," which he'd say while chewing on the end of a big cigar. I could almost imagine my guide Nestor saying it.

Nice one, Nestor. Have a cigar.

Sadly, I knew Frances was dying. I had the strangest feeling Uncle Alan would be collecting Frances when her time was due as her parents, though well into their eighties, would probably survive her.

The next evening, sitting in the physical circle in the dark, I mentioned this complicated sequence of events.

Keith took it all in stride. "You see, Ian. You were saying your energy's been low lately and you've found it difficult to connect with spirit. But once you've made the connection, it's always there. Sometimes it's weaker, sometimes it's stronger. But the link is never broken and they'll always find a way to get through. They always do."

34

Survivor

"I've spent my whole life searching, exploring, and wondering what it's all about."

Despite his many years in England, Charles Stevens still had a fruity Polish accent that added gravitas to his words. As he said "searching, exploring, and wondering," he screwed his face up as if experiencing considerable pain. His words were poignant because although some might say his search had taken him to the heights of spiritual insights, it had started from the depths of personal and global tragedy.

Sitting next to him at Ola and David's dining table, I was trying to assess his age. He'd been 16 when the Nazis had invaded Poland, which meant he was now about 83 years old. For a man who'd suffered severe privations as a youth, he looked very well. He sported a full head of wire-gray hair, side parted. He had clear, hazel eyes. His face often wore an inquiring expression, one naturally attributed to a lively intelligence. But it was also possibly due to being somewhat deaf in his right ear ("the Nazis shot at me and the bullet grazed my ear").

Sometimes you meet someone new but feel as if you've always known them. Charles was one of those people. Yet we couldn't have come from more different backgrounds.

Born Chaim Sieradzki, he had grown up in a well-off, middle class Polish Jewish family. His family had owned a well-known confectionery business. Well-educated and multi-lingual, Charles was seriously contemplating taking his religious studies further when war broke out. He managed to escape from his Nazi captors and headed east towards what he thought was the safe haven of Stalin's Russia. But the Communist worker's paradise that had beguiled so many young people of his generation was to prove a shameful lie. He was imprisoned in a Siberian gulag where he was tortured and pressed into hard physical labor under extremely brutal conditions. Repeated beatings to his head from the prison guards further damaged his hearing. The breakdown of the Hitler-Stalin pact allowed him his freedom as long as he agreed to join an expatriate Polish army brigade under British command. However, being Jewish, he experienced much anti-Semitism from his fellow Polish soldiers.

His brigade was shipped to South Africa and then to England. He'd already learned some English and, as he was young and bright, quickly improved his knowledge of the language. His language skills landed him a job with military intelligence. He found the English to be welcoming and friendly, so, after the war, he decided to settle in England and took an English name. Charles wanted to continue his education and managed to obtain a place at medical school. However, he didn't have enough money to fund his studies and had to leave after his second year. In the meantime, he learned that half his family had perished in the concentration camps.

Charles had always felt protected by a higher power while in the gulag but needed to make sense of this feeling. Why had so many died? What was the purpose of all this suffering? And how could a good God allow it to happen?

While he was establishing himself in the custom tailoring business, he spent nine years on a personal spiritual quest to reconcile his deep feelings of spiritual purpose with a self-evidently suffering humanity. This quest would take him far from his Orthodox Jewish roots. As I was to do many years later, he had traveled some extremely strange paths.

Spiritualism always thrives during times of great loss of life as it purports to offer something tangible, which for other religions is only theoretical—reunion with those who've passed on. After the war, Spiritualist churches were packed with the grief-stricken trying to establish contact with their departed loved ones. Finding little comfort in Orthodox Judaism, Charles found himself drawn to the Spiritualist movement and he was to visit many, now famous, mediums.

He and his wife, Rita, eventually had a séance with Bill Ohlson, a gifted physical medium.

"The trumpet levitated and I could hear the voices of my family. One by one they called out their names. These were Polish Jewish names. They were the people I knew. My family. My father. There was no way he could have faked this." Charles gripped my arm. "It was phenomenal!"

The spirit voice of his father provided Charles with even more evidence from beyond the grave.

"My father told me I had his watch. It was an old fob watch. I had no recollection of this and thought he was mistaken."

However, this proved to be correct when he and Rita discovered the watch in a storage box that hadn't been opened for years. Charles then remembered that his sister's husband had given him the watch when they'd re-established contact in France, towards the end of the war. The watch was nothing special and had come with some other, more valuable, family heirlooms. Consequently, he'd had no special reason to remember he'd kept it.

There was more. He and his wife were convinced spirits had materialized and walked around the séance room.

"They got me to tie Mr. Ohlson to his chair with very strong ropes. There was no way he could move as I had secured his legs and arms very tightly. And there was no way anyone could untie them. They had to be cut with a knife. The room wasn't in darkness, the light was dim but we could clearly see what was happening," explained Charles.

"You could see ectoplasm flowing out of the medium's nose and mouth. It was like a dense white mist which built up into spirit forms," continued Rita.

I was impressed they'd witnessed ectoplasm firsthand. A mysterious substance supposedly produced from the body of a materialization medium, ectoplasm is said to be used by spirits to build a semblance of their original physical forms. In this case, the spirit forms were some of Charles' deceased family members.

"Then a freshly cut rose with the dew still on it materialized in my lap!" added Rita.

Convinced there was more to life than just "eating, sleeping, and reproducing," Charles, ever the frustrated medical student, devoted himself to learning the principles of spiritual healing. He'd run a very successful healing circle for many years. His tailoring business and his wife's gift shop did well, and he gave any donations he received for his healing to charity. Charles' life was full but tragedy struck again. His daughter had a baby girl with a rare disease that caused her to have learning difficulties. As if that were not bad enough, his daughter subsequently died of cancer some years later. Anxious to help suffering humanity, Charles and Rita decided to give up most of their accumulated savings to establish a trust fund to further cancer research at the Hebrew University of Jerusalem. The university uses this to pay for the research activities of two scientists.

Sad at times, but not bitter, Charles still spent much of his time "searching, exploring, and wondering" about the meaning of life. He'd concluded that although "we cannot possibly know what it's all about," there was definitely a higher purpose to life. Well-versed in Hebrew scripture, he liked to debate with Orthodox Jews in Jerusalem about where he felt religion had gone wrong.

"You see, religion should be about *service*, not *services*," he said to me, with a smile. "But it has become debased and is now only about power."

"Do you still do any healing?" I asked.

Charles spread his palms and inclined his head to one side.

"Not as much as I'd like. I get a little tired now I'm older. But yes, I still see people who are sent to me. I've never charged, but if people want to make a donation to Norwood Children's Homes then I'm very grateful."

I thought long and hard. I didn't want to impose on him, but I had a strong feeling I was supposed to meet him for a particular reason.

I was hesitant. "Charles, I know two people who might benefit from your healing." I mentioned Frances and Catherine.

"It would be a pleasure to help these poor suffering ladies," he said. "In fact, I feel we were meant to meet so I can help them." He tilted his head inquiringly and said, "But, of course, you know this is how spirit works?"

I telephoned Catherine. She was having a bad time. She was due to start radiotherapy and had been fitted with a rather frightening plastic mask, which was to be used during her radiotherapy sessions. The mask went over her face and head. The radiotherapy technician would use this to help adjust the radiation beam to make sure it hit her tumor. She was dreadfully anxious but listened carefully when I told her about Charles.

"I can't promise you it will help, but I can't imagine it would do any harm. And, you know, I get the feeling I was meant to meet this guy, for your sake," I said.

Catherine was grateful.

"I'm so pleased you told me about him. He sounds very kind. Please let me have his details and I'll go and see him."

A week later, Catherine telephoned me to let me know she and Ted had visited Charles. He'd given her healing, which involved little more than a gentle laying on of hands. She found his personality enchanting and, if nothing else, certainly felt she'd received some emotional support at a difficult time. She would be seeing him weekly throughout her radiotherapy.

I met Barbara in the gym. I was pedaling away on an exercise bike when I spotted her coming into the large hall, clutching her water bottle. She seemed to be looking for someone. Evidently it was me, because as soon as she saw me she pointed, waved excitedly and dashed over.

She stood in front of my bike and stabbed her finger at me.

"Oh, well done! Well done!"

"What?" I said.

She continued stabbing her finger in the air as she uttered each word.

"You" stab "are" stab "definitely" stab "being" stab "guided" stab.

"Oh, come on then, out with it!" I said. I knew I wasn't going to discover what she was going on about without hearing the entire story.

She jumped onto the exercise bike next to me, fiddled about with its settings, bunched her hair up at the back with a scrunchie, and proceeded to pedal furiously.

"Do you remember I said I'd have a word with Shirley? I talked to her about Cathy and she thought Cathy might be helped if she saw a healer..."

"Oh, yes," I said. "Did you know I..."

"Shut up!" she said, excitedly. "Don't spoil my story. Yes, of course, I know! Anyway. We both thought Cathy's Ted would be a bit skeptical, and I didn't know whether or not I should even suggest it to her."

"And?" I asked

"Well, anyway, Shirley knows this healer and wanted me to suggest to Cathy that she goes to see him. So I took Cathy out for a drive."

She was really dragging this out. I hoped the punch line would be worth it. I tried to encourage her to give me the story a bit more quickly.

"So you and Cathy were in your car..." I prompted.

"Yes, and I was driving and... Anyway, we went past this house and I happen to know there's a healer who lives there. I thought I'd sort of use this to bring up the subject, to try to get Cathy to go and see Shirley's friend..."

"You mean Shirley's friend the healer lived at this house you were driving past?"

"No! That's a different healer! No, I just wanted to mention it to Cathy so I could talk about the other healer, Shirley's friend," she explained.

"Okay. So what happened next?"

"So, I said to her, 'Have you thought about seeing a healer? Shirley knows this chap.' And instead of her being all skeptical she says, 'Oh thanks, Barbara, but Ian's got me to see this lovely man. His name's Charles.' Now, Shirley's friend's also a Charles but there's no way, I thought, it could be him, so I said, 'That's funny. Shirley's friend's also named Charles.' And Cathy said, 'Not Charles Stevens, the Polish man?' and I almost ran the car into the curb. You see, it's the same Charles Stevens. How on earth do you know him?"

I told Barbara about how I'd been introduced to Charles. We looked at each other in stunned amazement. Shirley's sister had been friendly with Charles' wife, Rita, for at least 30 years. It seemed Catherine was destined to meet Charles, one way or another.

Not so my cousin Frances. She was unreceptive to the idea of seeing a healer. I wasn't surprised, as my entire family had never had much time for anything spiritual. I knew my profession could offer her only temporary respite. Her tumor had spread to her lungs and it was just a matter of time. I only hoped Uncle Alan would come to collect her when her time was due.

35

The Secret

"You ought to read this book, Ian." Keith tapped its glossy cover with a nicotine-stained index finger. "I got it for 50 pence in the charity shop," he added, grinning.

It was a slim book, with the cover designed to look like old parchment, bearing a large red wax seal. It was called *The Secret*. I glanced at it, flicked through it, and sniffed. It looked like some schmaltzy American "power of positive thinking" nonsense. I normally had no argument with positive thinking. In fact reading books like this had led me to learning about hypnosis. But lately I hadn't been feeling particularly positive.

We'd been going through major changes at work, with yet another National Health Service reorganization. I'd been seeing Catherine weekly for hypnosis to help her cope with her daily radiotherapy sessions, which had begun to take their toll. Her throat was sore and her tongue had large, painful ulcers on it. She'd lost a lot of weight. Frances' health was obviously failing and she now had tumor deposits in her brain. And there was still the usual unrelenting daily round of my patients to sort out. I needed a vacation and I was looking forward to going off to Austria for a couple of weeks.

Keith sensed my cynicism. "You really need to read this book. You've been a bit negative lately."

I promised I would. When I got home, I put it to one side. Maybe I shouldn't have, because what happened to me subsequently all started with a negative thought.

We were due to fly to Austria in two days time. I was getting dressed after a workout in the gym. As I put my glasses on, I was thinking about the first time I ever went to Austria on a school skiing trip when I was 16. I'd broken my glasses the week before and a very kind optician had delivered a new pair to my home the night before I was due to travel. I certainly wouldn't fancy breaking my glasses like that again, just before a holiday! With that thought, my glasses slipped from my hand and fell to the tiled changing-room floor. There was a tinkling sound as the right lens broke. Fortunately, I had a spare lens. I took this to my optician to have it fitted. While I was there, I had my reading prescription adjusted and ordered a new pair of glasses. I wasn't too upset about this incident; the prescription had needed adjusting for ages and this was an opportunity to get it done. My new glasses would be ready when I came back from my vacation.

My spare lens was fine for distance, but the reading prescription wasn't quite right. I was really only having a bit of trouble seeing the computer screen in my office. But as it was now the morning before my departure, I could manage.

There was a knock on my door. It was Kieran, the medical center's chiropodist.

"Ian, I hear you know some psychics," he said, standing uncertainly in the doorway.

"Quite a few, yes," I said.

Kieran sat down in one of my chairs.

"I'd like someone to do a clairvoyant reading for me. Can you suggest anyone you know?"

I thought of Barbara. I knew she'd be happy for me to send her some work, so I turned to the computer, requested a list of patients with her surname, found her name in the list, and gave him her phone number. I thought nothing more of it.

Our vacation in Austria was fantastic. Unusually, the lobby of our hotel had glass cabinets filled with books covering subjects such as paranormal phenomena, survival after death, and spirituality. It could have been the Austrian version of

Vestry Road Spiritualist Church library. We spent two weeks walking, cycling, and eating.

Back home from Austria, I was tired from the vacation. I'd noticed I'd often have minor accidents on return from vacation because of tiredness. This time I was determined not to have an accident. I had to take down a fence panel for the cable TV company to gain access to my connection point. Knowing my tendency to have accidents, I was extremely careful. The fence panel came off easily and I relaxed. I had one more job to do—fix Paul's bike. It should have been a cinch, as I just needed to re-thread a brake cable. No problem. But I cut the brake cable. I also cut a chunk of flesh from my left index finger. It was not good. There was a piece of skin missing. I would need stitches to close the wound. Having a wife who's a doctor was helpful; Punam drove me down to my clinic and put in three stitches. True to form, as I'd expected, I'd had my accident.

That evening, preparing for work the next day, I checked through my email. There was a cryptic message from Jacky, our new manager: "Hi Ian. Hope you enjoyed your vacation. I'm not sure if this is anything to do with you, but one of our patients telephoned us. Apparently, she received a strange phone call from a man claiming to be from the clinic asking for a clairvoyant reading. He said you had recommended him to her. Any idea what this is about? Can I leave it with you? Jacky."

At first, I couldn't imagine what had happened. But when I looked at the name Jacky had given me, I realized the patient, Cindy, had the same surname as Barbara. I'd obviously given Kieran the wrong phone number. Cindy's name would have been just below Barbara's. As I hadn't had the correct reading prescription in my glasses, I must have read the wrong line on the computer monitor. My simple mistake had left three people mystified: Cindy, who had absolutely no interest in anything psychic (as far as I knew); Kieran who hadn't expected such a frosty reception; and Barbara, whom I'd telephoned and told to expect a call from Kieran, which she'd never received.

It was now my first day back at work. That year, I sometimes used to cycle to work. When the weather was fine it was very pleasurable to do house calls on my bike, avoiding the busy roads and taking short cuts through local parks. I'd done a lot of cycling while on vacation and I thought I'd keep up my cycling fitness and leave the car at home. On second thought, now that I had stitches in my finger and was still worrying about the possibility of accidents, I decided to take the car. While I was at it, I put the book Keith had given me, *The Secret*, into the trunk. I hadn't read it, wasn't going to read it, and I planned to give it back to Keith the following Tuesday evening.

The first thing I did was telephone Cindy to apologize. She took it well and thought the whole thing was immensely funny. I would have to speak to Kieran later.

Leaving the medical center that morning, as I edged my car out into the main road, I hit another car that was going past. I still don't know how I did it. Luckily the damage was minor. My car's hood would need to be repainted, as would the nearside, rear wheel arch panel of the car I hit. The other driver, a Dutch tourist, was philosophical.

"These things happen," he said, as we swapped insurance details over a cup of coffee in my office.

That made two accidents.

I sat in my colleague Dr. Anthony Marks' room later that morning. I was having a moan. He commiserated with me about my cut finger and my damaged car. Then his phone rang. It was his wife. She'd just backed into another car while leaving a parking lot at the hospital where she worked as a nurse. This was getting infectious.

That evening I was at home having my evening meal when the phone rang. It was Anthony. I wondered what was wrong, as he rarely phoned me at home. His voice sounded strange, as if he was trying to suppress a giggle.

"What's the matter?" I asked.

"I just thought you'd like to know what happened to me this evening. I had to get some papers out of the filing cabinet to sort out Philippa's car. There was a sharp edge somewhere and I cut my finger. Philippa had to close the wound with steri-strips. It's the same finger as yours. The minute it happened, I just knew you'd want to hear about it."

This was all getting a bit out of control. I felt that someone, somewhere, was trying to tell me something, but I was just too dense to understand.

The following day, Tuesday, before my afternoon clinic, there was a nervous knock on my door. It was Kieran, the chiropodist, looking apologetic.

"Ian, I'm really sorry. I hope I didn't upset one of your patients, but when I phoned that lady whose number you gave me she hadn't got a clue what I was going on about."

I looked at Kieran sheepishly.

"Yeah. Sorry about that, Kieran," I said. "It was my fault. I gave you the wrong number. Here's the correct number."

He scribbled it down and looked at me.

"Ian, you look terrible. Is everything okay?"

I told him about my two accidents; how, in some mysterious way, I'd been expecting them; and how my accident-proneness seemed to have infected Anthony and his wife.

"You know what, Ian?"

"What?" I asked.

"There's a book you ought to read."

"What's that?" I asked. I should have known what he was going to say.

"It's called *The Secret*."

I must have given him a strange look, because he frowned and said, "What's wrong?"

"Hang on a minute," I said. "Don't go away." I jumped out of my chair and dashed to my car. I returned with the book and thrust it under his nose.

"You mean this?"

"Yes," he said.

I didn't give the book back to Keith that evening. Instead, I read it from cover to cover. I thought I probably ought to. The secret turned out to be that you attract what you think about. So watch your thinking. You bet!

One Tuesday evening, just after I'd finished reading *The Secret*, I was sitting in the kitchen at Vestry Road Spiritualist Church with Keith and June, waiting for the others to arrive.

Keith laughed like a drain when I gave him the book back and told him my story.

"So, what did you have to learn, then, do you think?"

"Well, I knew about the dangers of negative thinking. But I've been so tired lately I just got into the habit of expecting the worst."

"Sometimes we all forget and need to be reminded. I suppose that's why they wanted you to read the book."

"You mean my guides?"

"Who do you think? Yes. Remember, you've been low lately and it's been hard for them to get through. They told you they'd always find a way. They probably got me to buy the book so you could read it. Now, if you'd read the book when I told you to, maybe you wouldn't have had to learn your lesson the hard way. "

It sounded crazy. I thought it over. It was certainly odd,

though. And there seemed to be an underlying pattern and possibly a few symbolic links.

"You know what Keith? It's funny how it all started with me thinking about how I broke my glasses just before going to Austria as a kid. It's like there's a pattern. You know, glasses, seeing, seeing clearly, clairvoyance."

"Ooh, are those your new glasses?" asked June, who was half-listening to our conversation as she was reading the *Evening Standard*.

"Yes. Do you like them?"

June squinted at me. "Well, to be honest, they don't look much different from your old ones."

"Well, the color's different," I said. "These have a gold frame and the other ones were silver. And..." I took them off and peered short-sightedly at the frame, "I think they're a different make. Let's have a look."

I noticed there was tiny writing in white lettering on the frame. I squinted at it. The writing said, "Made in Austria."

36

A Natural Break

Towards the end of November 2007, I was at the open circle and got talking to a new attendee. In her sixties, Mary was an experienced medium who'd known Keith Hudson for many years. She had just dropped in to see how he was teaching us.

While I was sitting next to her, she leaned towards me and said, "You're going to be writing a book, very soon."

I'd been told something like this before. In fact, practically every experienced medium I'd ever met, including Keith, had given me the same message—one day I would write a book about my experiences. I had a few chapters on my computer I'd written the previous year, but I'd been too distracted by events to carry on. Mary was the only one to mention I was going to be writing a book "very soon." I dismissed what she'd said; it wasn't likely as I was much too busy.

The next day, while cycling to see a patient, I hit my left knee against a fence. I carried on cycling, but it became obvious I'd done something bad to my knee. I rested it over the weekend and had it X-rayed the following Monday. I'd broken my kneecap. Thankfully, it was just a hairline fracture. But it meant I had to take six weeks off work, as I had to keep my left leg straight all the time and wear a knee splint. There would be no more psychic circles for me for a while.

Just to be safe, I decided to finish writing this book. It's a wild and wacky world out there in the Twilight Zone, and I thought perhaps I ought to get writing before "they" sent the boys around the break the other kneecap. You just never know...

Lynn's psychic development had hit an obstacle, too.

Kevin had been taking Lynn out as his fledgling, and she'd gained a reputation for giving accurate and evidential messages. She'd even started to take her own bookings for demonstrations of clairvoyance.

Lynn's mother, Margaret, was 87 years old by then and had begun to "fade" somewhat. I'd already warned Lynn what to expect. About a month before I broke my kneecap, Margaret developed a chest infection and died peacefully in hospital, surrounded by her children.

If you think being a medium in some way protects you from the feelings of loss after a bereavement, think again. Whatever your beliefs, the loss of someone's physical presence is very hard to take. Lynn had to cancel her bookings. After all, she'd been Margaret's caregiver for the previous 11 years. The loss of her mother left a big hole in her life.

She was also going to lose her home.

Lynn had lived with Margaret in a local government authority rented house. She now had to give up this two-bedroom house and make an application for a single-persons' apartment. The inevitable paperwork required some medical input. I'd asked Lynn to make an appointment to see me so I could sort this out for her. Unfortunately, now I couldn't because I was stuck at home with my knee.

"Never mind, I'll see Dr. Marks," she said, when I phoned her to explain my predicament.

"Okay, Lynn. I'll let Anthony know you're coming and what he needs to do."

But I forgot to phone Anthony.

One morning, I was sitting at home nursing my sore knee and getting my notes in order for this book, when I suddenly had a very strong urge to phone Lynn. So I did.

"Ian, thanks for phoning," she whispered, "but I can't

speak now because I'm actually sitting in your waiting room waiting to see Dr. Marks."

"Okay, Lynn, I'll phone you back in 20 minutes," I said, then immediately phoned Anthony to let him know what to do about her paperwork. He'd been just about to call her in.

You know what? I'd really like to think it was Margaret on the Other Side giving me a nudge, reminding me to keep an eye on her daughter.

Epilogue

While I was out of action with my broken knee, Frances died peacefully in the North London Hospice late in the night of January 4, 2008. Maybe she's with Uncle Alan now. But Catherine received a clean bill of health from the hospital. And Lynn got the apartment she wanted. So, had her mother really contacted me from the Other Side to make sure Lynn's paperwork got through? Maybe I'd just got lucky. Or maybe I'd read Lynn's mind.

Or maybe our understanding of the true nature of reality, causality, time, and consciousness are completely out of whack with what it's really all about.

At least now I had plenty of time to think about it and wonder, as I sat at home with my leg propped up on a footstool in front of me, watching reruns and chat shows on daytime TV.

What had my four-year journey all been about? Had I really had a rattling and rolling ride through the hinterland of reality? Or had I simply experienced a very flamboyant mid-life crisis?

Whatever it was, it seemed to have ground to a painful halt. It took six weeks for my knee to heal. And, you know, perhaps I just really needed the rest.

One thing's for sure, though—everything in this book really happened. Other than that, I offer no conclusions and no explanations. Make of it what you will. Hopefully, if you've just crossed over into your own Twilight Zone, you might take some comfort in my stories.

I have many questions and absolutely no answers. Furthermore, I have a sneaking suspicion that if someone were to explain to me what it had all been about, I probably wouldn't understand it anyway.

I'm still not a Spiritualist.

Many of my medical colleagues think I'm completely crazy. My Spiritualist friends say I think too much.

It's tough being between two worlds...

Acknowledgments

I'd like to thank all the people, some of them possibly discarnate, in various different worlds, who helped me with this book.

In the New World

It's a long hard slog getting a book to publication. If rejection slips weren't electronic nowadays, I could paper a wall with them. I just couldn't get a publisher or an agent in the UK interested in my manuscript, even with Keith Bishop's help (and he seems to know everybody)—and even though this book deals with something very British indeed. I'm an English doctor working as a general practitioner (GP) in a large NHS medical practice. And you'd think that a GP who gets messages from his dead patients might be of some interest to a UK publisher. But, in fact, I got a better reception from Anomalist Books, an American publishing house. That's why this book, which is set in the UK and was originally written in British English, is now in American English. I've had to use terms that would be more familiar to my American readers than my British readers. Many Americans might not know what a GP is. They'd certainly find use of the word "surgery" to indicate a building thoroughly confusing. This has given me a new perspective on British English words I'd previously just taken for granted. So, God bless America, God bless Anomalist Books, and God bless my editor, Patrick Huyghe.

In my world

Special thanks go to Keith Bishop and Lynn, who got me into this mess in the first place. I'd also like to thank Dave Godfrey, who gave me good advice when I was thrashing around wondering what was happening to me. Every doctor

269

should have patients like Keith, Lynn, and Dave. But I'd also like to thank all my patients who helped me on my strange journey. Some of them are mentioned in my book, but there are scores of others who encouraged me, listened to me, and even traveled with me, at least part of the way. I'd like to give special thanks to Linda Beckinsale and her daughter, Cheryl. They may not be in this book, but they played an important subsequent part in my journey and gave me the confidence to carry on. Sadly, Lynda Nixon, who is in the book, is no longer with us.

Of course, another Keith deserves my gratitude. This book would not exist if it were not for Keith Hudson. Keith has the capacity to both educate and thoroughly confuse at the same time. It's a wonderful gift.

I'd also like to thank yet another Keith: Keith Miller. He'll know why. And I'd like to say, "God bless!" to the congregation and committee of Vestry Road Spiritualist Church, a safe haven in the Twilight Zone and a credit to the Spiritualist movement.

I must mention my medical and nursing colleagues and all the staff at Eagle House Surgery. I can't imagine any other medical practice putting up with a doctor who suspects that he might be able to communicate with his deceased patients, and then decides to tell everyone about it.

Thanks also to my family. Punam had to put up with all the hours I spent at the keyboard, and my constant requests to read the bits of my manuscript I wasn't happy with. My sons had to put up with a dad who, quite frankly, went a little strange, but instead of going into recovery, decided to embrace it. Not easy when you're a teenager.

In the media world
I'd like to acknowledge the encouragement I received from

Sarah Hartley and Angela Levin, both of the *Mail On Sunday*. When you're pushing your professional boundaries almost to breaking point, it's slightly terrifying to contemplate what a newspaper might say if it found out. Well, one newspaper did find out—and it was fun!

Likewise *Take a Break's Fate & Fortune* magazine's Clair Stretton deserves a mention.

Richard Alwyn and Rachel Noar of Ronachan Films also had a part in this. Like me, they were parachuted into a bizarre world that seldom seemed to make sense. Unlike me they had to make a coherent TV program about it in four months! I found their comments very helpful, and they gave me a platform to tell some of my stories, as did Steve Gilmour of Talk Radio Europe.

In the spirit world
Is there anybody there?

Well, I did challenge you guys, didn't I? I said, "Prove to me you're real by getting my book published!"

Look what you've done.

Thanks.